D0624072

The Computerized Society

Other Publications:
MYSTERIES OF THE UNKNOWN
TIME FRAME
FIX IT YOURSELF
FITNESS, HEALTH & NUTRITION
SUCCESSFUL PARENTING
HEALTHY HOME COOKING
LIBRARY OF NATIONS
THE ENCHANTED WORLD
THE KODAK LIBRARY OF CREATIVE PHOTOGRAPHY
GREAT MEALS IN MINUTES
THE CIVIL WAR
PLANET EARTH
COLLECTOR'S LIBRARY OF THE CIVIL WAR
THE EPIC OF FLIGHT
THE GOOD COOK
WORLD WAR II
HOME REPAIR AND IMPROVEMENT
THE OLD WEST

This voluume is one of a series that examines
various aspects of computer technology
and the role computers play in modern life.

UNDERSTANDING COMPUTERS

The Computerized Society

BY THE EDITORS OF TIME-LIFE BOOKS
TIME-LIFE BOOKS, ALEXANDRIA, VIRGINIA

Contents

Taming the Mainframe

Ed Pecorella first realized something was wrong on a hectic day in January 1985. Pecorella, director of the Internal Revenue Service center in Ogden, Utah—one of ten regional offices in the United States to which tax returns are mailed—spied a young clerk amid a jam of carts groaning under mounds of stacked paper. "How's it going?" Pecorella asked.

The clerk glared at him. "You really want to know?" she said. "I can't find anything. We're out of control."

The piles of paper surrounding her were unprocessed tax returns, early warnings of a bureaucratic disaster that was about to engulf the U.S. tax system. Facing an onslaught of some 178 million 1984 returns, the IRS was confronting its ultimate nightmare—computer failure.

Computers are the heart and soul of U.S. tax processing. The previous November, just weeks before the start of the filing season, the IRS had pulled the plug on outmoded equipment that had been at the core of its operation since the 1960s. At work was a brand-new $131-million system: ten powerful Sperry 1100/84 mainframes at the service centers linked to an eleventh machine at the tax bureau's central computing facility in Martinsburg, West Virginia.

Problems with the hastily installed equipment appeared almost immediately. The computers at the Atlanta and Memphis centers mysteriously refused to start when they were turned on and had to be returned to Sperry for repairs. At the remaining centers, tape drives used for reading tax data broke down repeatedly, and other malfunctions were so frequent that some parts of the system could operate at only half the speed needed. Operators found they could not even rely on a program designed to allow computers that crashed to resume processing where they left off: Each time the system went down, the operators had to start again from scratch.

By the April 15 filing deadline, with more than 19 million returns pouring in during the final week, the tax centers were hopelessly behind schedule. Hundreds of millions of dollars in refunds went unpaid, dunning letters arrived at the homes of innocent citizens whose tax payments had been filed but not processed, and a mountain of inquiries remained unanswered. In a widely reported incident that seemed to symbolize the nightmare, bundles of returns were found in the rest-room wastebaskets of the Philadelphia center—apparently thrown out by overwhelmed IRS employees.

The 1985 tax-return crisis (remedied the following year by the installation of additional computers) was one of the most spectacularly public computer failures of all time—and a sobering reminder of just how dependent on these electronic wizards modern society has become. Like most large organizations that have computerized their operations over the past four decades, the Internal Revenue Service no longer has any other means of conducting its business. It could no more switch to old-fashioned manual accounting methods than a driver whose automobile has broken down can whistle up a horse-drawn cab. Just as earlier in the century the world came to depend on the internal-combustion engine, contemporary society cannot function without computers.

Like the IRS, other agencies of the federal government depend utterly on computers. Without access to the information stored in its vast electronic files, the government could not pay Social Security or veterans' benefits, maintain an army, or even hold an election. A malfunctioning computer can shut down a factory, stop the generation of electricity at a utility plant, or bring a city's subway to a halt. If the computers that operate our communications systems were to fail, telephones would fall silent and newspapers would fail to publish. Without computer-controlled radar, airplanes might collide in midair; without the computers that regulate traffic signals, automobiles in major cities would be immobilized. Computers solve the engineering equations needed to design our highways, bridges, and skyscrapers; they are behind the sophisticated diagnostic equipment of modern medicine. On any day, a dozen or more tiny computers may be at work in the typical American home—controlling the devices that cook our food, wash our dishes, and sew our clothes; providing entertainment in our videocassette recorders; tirelessly keeping time on wrists; and amusing our children by operating toy robots. At the bank, in the supermarket, and at the office, the school, and the library, computers are so commonplace that unless one calls attention to itself by breaking down, they pass almost unnoticed.

All of this has come to pass in a remarkably short period of time—little more than four decades of breathtaking technological progress. Today, the computing power of the first large-scale digital computer, the ENIAC—a behemoth of the 1940s that weighed thirty tons and cost close to half a million dollars—can be found on a microchip small enough to balance on a fingertip and so cheap that it can be used in a child's doll. A high-school student's personal computer is thirty to forty times faster than that earlier machine. A modern supercomputer exceeds its speed by more than a thousand times. If equivalent progress had occurred in automotive technology, you could now buy a Rolls-Royce for about $2.75. It would get three million miles a gallon, have enough horsepower to propel an ocean liner, and be fast enough to cross the continental United States in less than five minutes. If the car were miniaturized to the degree that computers have been reduced in size, the little limo could be driven through the eye of a needle.

At the most basic level, any computer—whether it is a giant mainframe processing tax returns or the microprocessor in a wristwatch—can perform only a single act: switching electrical voltage on and off at lightning speed. These pulses are directed into meaningful activity by the instructions contained in computer software, most of which is aimed at specific applications. With different applications programs, the same computer can shift chameleon-like from role to role—one moment calculating an accountant's spreadsheet or drawing up a contract, the next playing a game of chess. But the machine's true identity is determined by another class of software—called an operating system—that tells it how to manage its activities no matter what kind of job it is doing.

An operating system acts as the computer's internal government. It is made up of an integrated collection of complex programs that control all of the machine's resources, from its labyrinthine logic circuits and memory to its printers, keyboards and display screens. The operating system is loaded into the computer every time the machine is turned on and acts as a full-time resident manager, issuing the detailed instructions the machine requires to do everything from shuttling pieces of data in and out of memory to displaying one glowing character on a terminal screen. Without an operating system, the thousands of such commands that may be needed to complete a single computing job would have to be included in each application program—which would be like instructing a human worker to perform a specific task and at the same time explaining to him exactly how to breathe, work his limbs, and keep his heart beating.

That, in fact, was much the situation faced by users of the first computers. Their machines ran without operating systems and were so difficult to program that practical use was severely limited. But as computers evolved, operating systems evolved with them, making computers more economical and easier to use even as the machines grew more and more powerful and complex. In consequence, computers were harnessed for an ever-widening range of applications.

There are many types of operating systems. Each determines what is known as a computing environment. For example, the Sperry computers at the IRS—as well as the computers at many other large institutions such as banks, insurance companies, or universities—are supervised by operating systems that can create a so-called batch environment, in which large volumes of data are processed continuously at high speed without human interaction after the work is under way. A different environment, known as multiuser on-line, allows a number of users to tap into and interact with one computer simultaneously, as when travel agents make airline reservations, or department-store clerks check their customers' credit status. Some on-line systems, characterized as "fault-tolerant," include elaborate safeguards to protect data from accidental loss or damage in the event of a computer failure. Fault-tolerant systems give banks, for instance, the confidence to transfer millions of dollars from city to city or over oceans without fear that the money will vanish if a computer fumbles. Beginning in the early 1970s, a group of operating systems designed for personal computers made it possible for people outside large institutions to use computers cheaply and easily, leading to the subsequent boom in the small machines.

Today, virtually the only computers that do not use some kind of operating system are individual microprocessors dedicated solely to a single application such as selecting the stitches on a sewing machine or setting the lens aperture of a camera. Yet even these tiny computers on a chip have operating-system-like self-management and control instructions etched into their microscopic circuits along with the commands that dictate their limited activities. For all other computers, the operating system is perhaps the closest thing there is to a soul in the machine. Tireless, capable, and largely unseen, it has played a pivotal role in the computer revolution. The computerization of society has been the story of the socialization of the computer—and that in many ways is the story of the development of computer operating systems.

EMERGENCE OF THE ELECTRONIC BRAINS

When the first electronic computers emerged from university and military laboratories in the late 1940s and early 1950s, visionaries proclaimed them the harbingers of a second industrial revolution that would transform business, government, and industry. But few laymen, even if they were aware of the machines, could see the connection. Experts, too, were skeptical. Not only were

An Obstacle Course for Tax Returns

A computerless IRS could not function. An army of clerks and examiners would be necessary to process manually the nearly 200 million tax returns that inundate the agency's ten regional service centers each year. Even if such a work force could be assembled, it would be unwieldy, expensive, and a source of errors guaranteed to raise a clamor among taxpayers.

Since the introduction of data processing to the agency in the early 1960s, computers have figured most prominently in the IRS system known as pipeline processing *(right)*. This operation, a mixture of manual and computerized procedures, handles as many as seven million returns a week during peak periods.

At the beginning of the pipeline circuit are ten regional service centers, where tax returns are mailed. At the end of the pipeline is the IRS's National Computer Center (NCC), situated in Martinsburg, West Virginia. There, tax data forwarded from all service centers are posted to taxpayer accounts in the master files, which contain three-year tax histories for each taxpayer. The NCC runs the information through a host of computer processes to ferret out duplicate claims for refunds, to analyze data for demographic research projects, and even to apply a secret formula that helps IRS agents determine whether a return warrants an audit.

Anomalous returns—those that are incomplete or that fail the computer's tests—are ejected from the pipeline into the hands of expert tax examiners. Working at a terminal, an examiner can call a faulty tax return to the screen, fix some kinds of errors—incorrect addition or subtraction, for example—then reinsert the return into the pipeline. However, incomplete returns usually require correspondence with the taxpayer and must go to the beginning of the pipeline. Some rejections occur as late as the NCC checkpoint. These so-called unpostables—returns with invalid or nonexistent social security numbers, for instance—are returned to their respective service centers for follow-up.

Although computer advances have been incorporated in the pipeline, machines throughout the system continue to employ one of the oldest modes of computer operation—batch processing. This method was chosen, not because of computer limitations, but in order to keep track of individual tax returns. Returns travel through the pipeline in batches of two thousand or so, making individual returns easier to locate amid the millions that each year fill the nation's coffers.

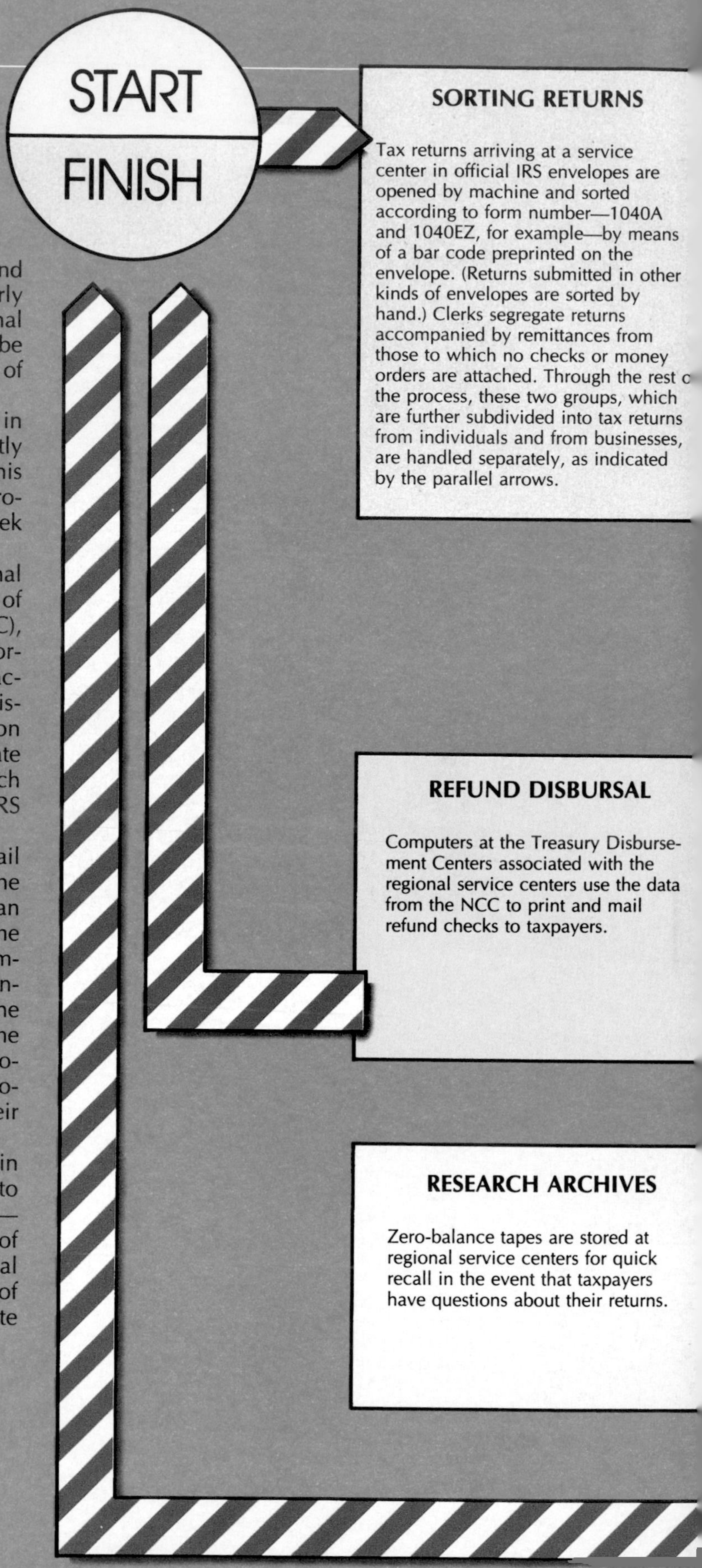

START

FINISH

SORTING RETURNS

Tax returns arriving at a service center in official IRS envelopes are opened by machine and sorted according to form number—1040A and 1040EZ, for example—by means of a bar code preprinted on the envelope. (Returns submitted in other kinds of envelopes are sorted by hand.) Clerks segregate returns accompanied by remittances from those to which no checks or money orders are attached. Through the rest o the process, these two groups, which are further subdivided into tax returns from individuals and from businesses, are handled separately, as indicated by the parallel arrows.

REFUND DISBURSAL

Computers at the Treasury Disbursement Centers associated with the regional service centers use the data from the NCC to print and mail refund checks to taxpayers.

RESEARCH ARCHIVES

Zero-balance tapes are stored at regional service centers for quick recall in the event that taxpayers have questions about their returns.

BLOCKS AND BATCHES

Clerks check the amount paid against the tax due for each return, noting any discrepancy on the tax form. Returns are grouped into blocks of 100, each return and its accompanying check or money order receiving a locator number. The numbered checks are then deposited, while the returns are assembled into batches of about twenty blocks. Returns not accompanied by remittances are divided into temporary batches pending further review.

REVIEW OF RETURNS

Before being converted into computer data, all returns are reviewed for completeness, legibility, and the presence of a signature. Any returns that fail this examination are rejected. Upon passing this scrutiny, returns without remittances are assigned locator numbers and grouped into final batches.

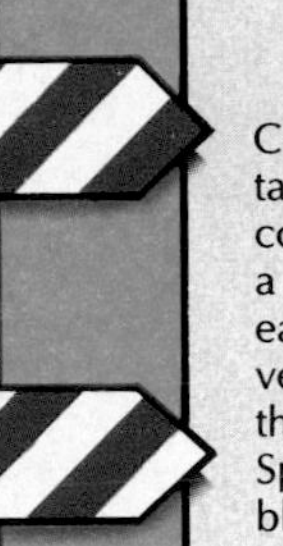

ENTERING THE DATA

Clerks manually enter data from the tax-return forms into an on-line computer data base. To prevent errors, a second clerk reenters key lines from each return. When the two clerks' versions match, the computer approves the return for further processing. Special codes identify the batch and block to which a return belongs so it can be retrieved later.

ARITHMETIC CHECK

Batch by batch, the computer checks each return to verify the taxpayer's arithmetic. Returns with correct calculations are copied onto magnetic tapes called "good tapes," which are forwarded to the master file *(below, left)*. For other returns, the computer calculates discrepancies and records them on balance-due or error tapes. Information printed from error tapes is reviewed by tax examiners; balance-due tapes are the basis for computer-generated notices to the taxpayers.

THE NATIONAL LEVEL

Good tapes from the ten regional service centers arrive at the NCC, where the data is merged, then sorted by social-security number or employer-identification number. Next, return data is posted to master-file accounts. During this process, social-security and employer numbers are verified. Tapes of returns due refunds are forwarded to the Treasury Department's six Regional Disbursement Centers *(left, top arrow)*. A tape of returns bearing unverifiable social-security or employer numbers is sent to each service center, along with a tape of zero-balance returns, those accompanied by the correct tax payments *(center arrow)*. After tax season, the NCC cross-checks financial information supplied by organizations such as banks and employers against the master-file accounts. Taxpayers for whom this comparison reveals unreported income receive computer-generated notices from the NCC *(bottom arrow)*.

computers huge, expensive, one-of-a-kind devices designed for performing abstruse scientific and military calculations, such as cracking codes and calculating missile trajectories, they were also extremely difficult to handle.

A computer demanded constant attention from skilled teams of engineers and technicians. These operators had to devise each of the computer's moves in excruciating detail, with "machine code"—the binary language of ones and zeros—equivalent to the computer's internal electronic traffic of on-off pulses. Directions were given to the machine by flipping switches or by plugging and unplugging hundreds of cables. In addition to steering the computer through its calculations step by laborious step, the first computer operators were also obliged to initiate and supervise every other action the machine performed, from accepting data and instructions to providing the finished results—jobs that today are handled automatically by operating systems.

The first attempts to improve productivity came in the early 1950s with development of rudimentary computer languages, in which simple mnemonics—short, easy-to-recall combinations of letters—could be substituted for the ones and zeros of machine code when a computer programmer drew up instructions for the computer. Libraries of prewritten program instructions for commonly used command sequences—called subroutines—relieved programmers of the chore of writing every instruction from scratch. Programs were composed in a form of notation called assembly language, in which a short mnemonic directly represented a specific instruction to the machine. A separate program called an assembler converted the mnemonics into the binary sequences that the machine could understand.

The relative convenience of assembly language was one of the selling points of the first commercial computers. Remington Rand's UNIVAC, which appeared in 1951, and the series of IBM computers that debuted in 1953 all had assembly languages written specifically for them. Programming was still not an easy job. Assembly language demanded an intimate knowledge of the machine, and as much as a year was needed to train the dozen or so engineers that were associated with a single computer. Once trained, those experts had to spend months programming the machine before they could get any useful work out of it. Nonetheless, the demand for computers proved greater than either of the two manufacturers had anticipated. IBM—which leased its costly creations—was particularly successful with three early computers and jumped ahead of its lone rival to secure the lead in the nascent industry.

The IBM and UNIVAC customers fell into two broad categories. The first were classed as "business" users, typically large companies whose traditional manual and mechanical accounting methods were being stretched to the breaking point by growing masses of payroll, accounting, inventory, and billing data. Government agencies such as the Census Bureau, the IRS, and the Social Security Administration, all coping with swelling mounds of paperwork generated by an exploding post-World War II population, were included in the business category—and were among the most eager to obtain the new computers. The second group, "scientific" users, was made up principally of scientists in research laboratories and engineers in the design departments of aircraft, automobile, and chemical companies.

Computers quickly proved they could earn their keep for all of these customers. The IBM 701, designed primarily for scientific and engineering applications, not only scored a solid hit in the laboratories of companies such as Lockheed and Monsanto Chemical but proved it could pull its weight in their front offices as well, assembling financial data, preparing quarterly reports, and processing payrolls. When Prudential Life replaced 86 pieces of old-fashioned punch-card accounting and calculating equipment with a single IBM 702 (a business-oriented version of the 701), it found it could service 80,000 policies a day and send out ten million premium notices each year with 200 fewer clerks than the job needed before.

IBM's 650, a smaller, less powerful alternative to the 701 and 702, was an even greater success. Rugged, versatile, and inexpensive (renting for $3,000 to $4,000 a month, as opposed to the $24,000-a-month cost of the 701), the 650 was the first runaway seller of the computer industry. Eventually installed at more than 1,800 locations, it was the machine most instrumental in computerizing American businesses—from insurance and sales to missile development and oil refining. Chrysler Corporation was so taken with the 650 that it ordered three, two for research and one for payroll and cost accounting.

Yet despite the great strengths of computers, pioneering users soon became all too aware of inefficiencies in the way the machines worked and the manner in which they were used.

A WASTE OF RESOURCES

Whether they were evaluating equations or processing payrolls, UNIVAC and the IBM 701, 702 and 650 all worked in basically the same manner. Then, as now, a computer consisted of two main components: a central processing unit (CPU) and an internal memory. The CPU harbored all of the machine's arithmetic, logic, and control circuitry—in effect its working brain. It solved problems by following a program, a sequence of precise instructions that told it how to manipulate a related set of data. The memory—called the primary or main memory—held those instructions as well as data for retrieval by the CPU.

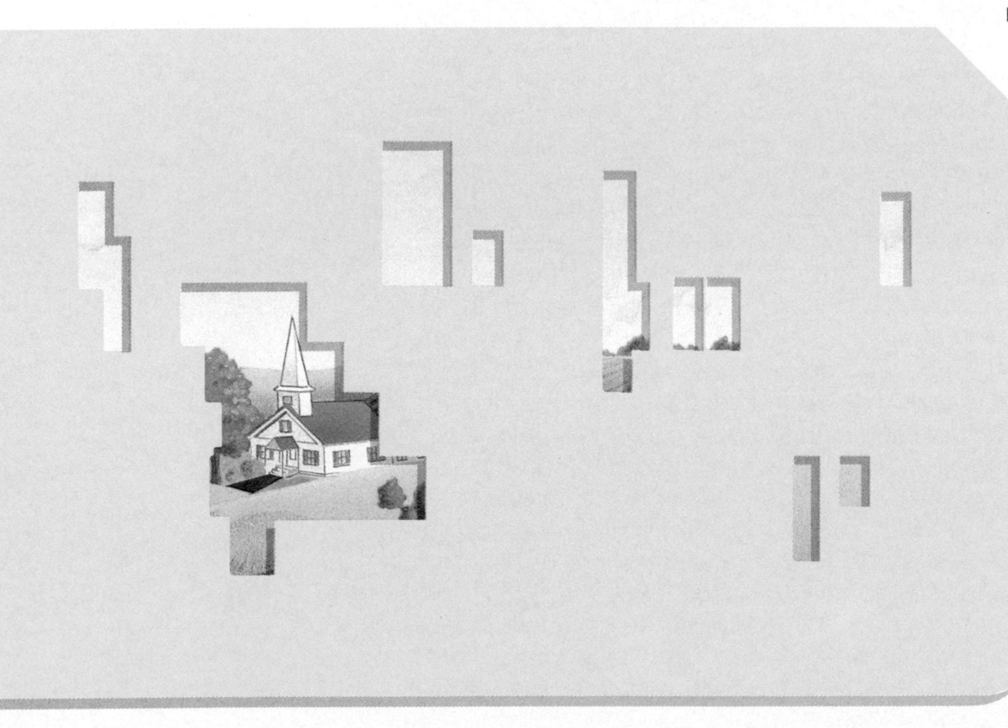

Main memories had a limited capacity; the 701's memory, for example, could hold only 2,048 thirty-six-bit "words," each word representing six alphanumeric characters. So computers were also equipped with external storage devices—magnetic recording tape or cylindrical metal drums, referred to as secondary memory—that provided a much larger backup reservoir for data. Typically, external storage was used as a repository for large files containing such information as payroll records or lists of customers. During long data-processing jobs, the information was shuttled into main memory as needed.

Programs were prepared by using a keypunch to code instructions and data into patterns of tiny holes in stiff, envelope-size cards—the same type of punched cards that had been used for decades with mechanical office equipment. All the cards for a given computing job were fed to an electromechanical device called a card reader, which transformed the punched holes into electronic pulses, sending a train of electronic bits—binary digits—directly into the computer. On arrival, the pulse trains were routed by the CPU into memory, each instruction or piece of data having been assigned to its own unique memory location.

To perform a calculation, the CPU fetched one piece of data from memory at a time, performed the necessary arithmetic, and returned the intermediate results to memory. When the series of computations were finished, the CPU directed the results to a printer or a card punch machine.

While perfectly straightforward and logical, this process wasted the computer's greatest asset, the blinding speed of its central processing unit. At the beginning of a job, the processor could do nothing but direct electronic traffic until the card reader had scanned the set of cards in its hopper and put the instructions and the data for a job into memory. It was similarly hobbled at the end of a job as the results trickled out by way of some sluggish output device such as a card punch. This was a glaring handicap. The 701's CPU, for example, could compute at the brisk rate of 16,000 instructions per second. But its card reader dawdled along at a top rate of 150 cards a minute. Thus, programs written with one instruction per card were read into the machine at a pace more than 6,000 times slower than the rate at which the CPU could process the information. The card punch was even tardier, producing only 100 cards a minute.

In most computer installations, this basic imbalance in the way the machine operated was compounded by long waits between jobs and substantial difficulties in getting programs to work correctly in the first place. As Bob Patrick, a 701 programmer with a Fort Worth aircraft manufacturer, Convair, put it: "Programming in the early 1950s could best be described as organized chaos."

In 1951, Patrick was a restless 22-year-old second lieutenant at California's Edwards Air Force Base. A chance to take a UCLA course in operating IBM's Card-Programmed Electronic Calculator (CPC)—an electronic calculating machine that preceded IBM's first commercial computers—struck him as a "great opportunity" to spend weekends in Los Angeles and meet girls. The experience he gained as a result of that casual decision landed him a civilian job two years later at Convair, where he entered the ranks of what would become the first professional computer programmers.

His job was to use a CPC, and later a newly acquired 701, to analyze mathematical design models for the B-58 Hustler, a delta wing, supersonic bomber destined for the Strategic Air Command. The work involved translating an engineer's design of an aircraft component—such as the skeleton of the wing—into a mathematical model, then testing the model in computerized simulations of flight conditions such as varying altitude and air speed. Each set of conditions involved literally thousands of computations to determine the force on the component.

For Convair's twenty-odd young programmers ("a bunch of miscellaneous college graduates," as Patrick described them), preparing programs meant a long, arduous process of trial and error. Only about 20 percent of their time with the computer was spent churning out answers to engineering problems. The other 80 percent was devoted to running what they called "test shots," in which kinks in developing programs were uncovered through debugging—a process that often left Patrick and his colleagues looking less like the advance troops of a technological revolution than a bumbling corps of Keystone Cops.

Programmers were generally allowed fifteen minutes on the machine for each test shot. They scheduled time in the computer's stark, climate-controlled quarters by signing up on a first-come, first-served waiting list. Then, with card decks in hand, they lined up outside the computer room like hungry diners waiting for a table in a crowded restaurant.

When a programmer finished, the next person in line would dash into the room and start setting up his job—a frantic round of readying the necessary input and output devices, setting program control switches, and feeding cards into the card reader. If all went well, a deft programmer could set up the computer and load a typical deck of 300 cards in about five minutes. If things did not go smoothly—if a programmer fumbled or neglected to flip the necessary switches, or if the card reader jammed—the set-up process could drag on for ten minutes. "Or worse," recalled Patrick years later, "your time ran out and the next guy took the machine." As a result, the computer spent much more time waiting for work than it did computing.

GENESIS OF AN OPERATING SYSTEM

To get more useful work out of the machine, programmers began devising ways to save time—developing standardized set-up routines and teaming up to help one another start each job. But for Patrick, impatient to test his programs, these efficiencies were not enough. The computer was still hobbled by its mechanical input/output equipment and was still forced to stand idle between jobs.

Patrick began to experiment with ways to speed up the process. His ideas centered around a pioneering computer language called Speedcode, developed for the 701 by a young IBM designer named John Backus and supplied free of charge with the computer. Speedcode was a language interpreter, a piece of software that translated a program written in English-like commands into machine code, one line at a time as the program ran. Unlike assembly language, which required as many as four separate instructions to perform a simple task such as adding two numbers, Speedcode could accomplish the same thing with one pseudoinstruction—converted into four or more inside the computer. It also included a number of additional features designed to make programming go faster, such as ready-made commands for such predictable chores as controlling input and output devices.

Most programmers—including nearly all of those at Convair—spurned Speedcode because it took up almost half of the computer's main memory, leaving less room for their calculations, and because its interpretive routines slowed down the execution of programs, making them run anywhere from two to fifteen times longer than equivalent assembly-language programs. But Patrick considered this time discrepancy negligible when compared to the number of hours Speedcode saved otherwise. In one week, he could write a program that would take four weeks to compose in assembly language. Even though the finished program might require a hour to run rather than ten minutes, he had the solution to a given engineering problem weeks ahead of other programmers. "I could have results on a designer's desk while others were still punching cards."

Soon he began to explore ways to gain even more time by exploiting a Speedcode feature that directed the computer to copy programs and data from main memory onto the computer's magnetic drum or its tape drives. At the time, the 701's four tape units were used mainly to store data—such as atmospheric-condition tables—that was used for certain engineering calculations. Since all four were rarely in use at one time, Patrick could have a free tape unit for himself, and he began incorporating into his programs Speedcode routines that automatically copied his work onto tape whenever he loaded a test program card deck into the computer for the first time.

As a result, when it was Patrick's turn to use the machine again, he could quickly shift the program he needed from tape into the computer's main memory rather than having to load it anew from cards. This meant he could now debug his programs faster than the other programmers. To correct an error or alter a routine, he fed the computer only those cards needed to make the change.

This strikingly simple process reduced his standard program-loading time from three minutes to ten seconds. Patrick found he could scoot into the computer room, run his program, and get out with the results in less than three minutes—often operating the computer while other programmers were still struggling with their card decks.

"I got a test shot whenever I wanted just by squeezing in on the schedule," he remembered years later. "I was getting four and five shots a day when others were lucky to get two." His production runs took longer, but Patrick's total machine time was still only 25 percent that of any other programmer.

In mid-1954, Patrick moved to General Motors Research in Michigan, taking his freewheeling methods with him. Even though he was now programming design tests of gas turbines for the FireBird race car, his performance was much the same as when he had been working on bomber wings: He spent notably less time on the computer than his colleagues and produced finished programs and results much more quickly than purist assembly-language users.

Shortly before Patrick arrived at GM, IBM announced a successor to the 701. This was the 704, with a main memory twice as capacious as its predecessor's and a processor that was at least twice as fast. Patrick was assigned to a team studying ways a 704 could be used at GM. In mulling over how the resources of the new 704 should be managed, he crystallized his experiences and theories into a blueprint for the first recognized computer operating system.

A THREE PHASE OPERATING SYSTEM

At the center of Patrick's scheme was a trio of specialized devices developed by IBM for its business-oriented 702 computers: a card reader that transferred punched-card data directly onto magnetic tape without using the main computer as an intermediary, and a card punch and printer that similarly took information directly from tape. IBM had designed the stand-alone machines to help businessmen store and retrieve large data files. But GM reckoned it could employ them just as effectively for engineering applications.

Patrick's plan was to divorce the computer totally from clattering card machines and printers; the CPU would communicate only with the far speedier tape machines. Furthermore, he proposed to eliminate manual set-up time between individual jobs by loading a collection of jobs on a single tape and then feeding them to the computer so that they were processed one after the other, without interruption.

In November 1955—fourteen months before the new 704 was due to arrive at GM's suburban Detroit technical center—Patrick presented his ideas to a Boston meeting of SHARE, an organization of IBM users that met periodically to swap technical know-how. There he ran into Owen Mock, an engineer from North American Aviation who had been thinking along the same lines. The two agreed to work together to write the commands that would orchestrate the flow of jobs in and out of the 704.

Fourteen months later, they had put together what they called the three-phase operating system, or the GM-NAA I/O system, as it came to be known in the computer world. It was a package of integrated programs divided into three parts—input, execution, and output—under the control of a group of supervisory commands called the monitor.

The system formalized a computer-use method called batch processing—so named because a number of computing jobs were put together as a single batch, in much the same way that a batch of cookies are prepared for baking. Outside of the main computer room, the card-to-tape reader transferred information from several programmers' card decks, one programmer's stack at a time, to a single

input tape. This produced a magnetic replica of the cards—a series of instructions and data written in programming mnemonics and decimal numbers. The tape containing the batch of jobs was then carried into the computer room, hung on a tape unit attached to the 704, and its information fed to the computer. Guided by the monitor commands and the input-phase software, the CPU then used conversion routines to change the decimal material into binary instructions and data, which were transferred to a second tape. This completed the first phase.

During the second phase, the CPU processed each job in turn, sending results to a third tape, until the entire batch was completed. In phase three, processed results of all the jobs were read back into the machine, converted back into decimal, and transferred to a fourth and final tape. Then, while the computer began anew, starting phase one on the next batch, the decimal output tape was taken out of the computer room and its results fed to a printer or card punch.

At GM, the streamlined method of processing transformed the formerly chaotic process of running a computer into a smooth assembly-line procedure that rivaled those in the automaker's manufacturing plants. The computer was turned over to professional operators, whose job was merely to ensure that the machine always had a new input tape to read and a fresh output tape on which to store results. Other than that, said Patrick, "The operator doesn't have to do anything except watch to make sure the damn thing doesn't catch on fire." And unless the computer did in fact break down, it literally never stopped during a typical nine-hour shift.

The results were eye-popping. IBM had promised that the 704's processor would work twice as fast as the 701's. But at GM, with the novel operating system in place, the 704's throughput—the amount of work it could complete in a given time period—was twenty times that of the 701. Reported Patrick: "With the 701, you might do thirty jobs a day; on the 704, with this operating system, you could get 600 jobs a day."

Over the following months, the three-phase operating system was distributed free to SHARE members (in those days, such programs were not viewed as commercial products), and it quickly took root at some twenty 704 installations in addition to General Motors and North American Aviation. In 1956, a SHARE committee was formed to design a more advanced operating system for the 704's successor. After IBM formally announced the new machine, the IBM 709, in January 1957, the computer maker took over development of the SHARE Operating System (SOS) from the group.

Increasingly, IBM recognized that one of the keys to selling computers was to provide software that would help prospective buyers use their machines more easily. In that pragmatic vein, the company had already invested heavily in the development of programming languages. That spring, a team of software designers headed by Speedcode creator John Backus was putting the finishing touches on FORTRAN, a new programming language aimed at the scientific community. FORTRAN, the first widely distributed high-level language (high-level meaning that it approximates human language), was designed to allow scientists and engineers to use computers without depending on professional assembly-language programmers. Operating systems like the proposed SOS, with the potential for dramatically improving computer-room efficiency, could only make the machines even more attractive to customers.

A COMPUTER FOR BIG BOOKKEEPING JOBS

Initially, there was somewhat less interest in developing equivalent software for computers that were to be used by businessmen rather than scientists or engineers. COBOL, the first popular high-level language for business use, did not appear until 1960, and no operating systems as such were developed specifically for business-oriented computers like the IBM 702. At IBM, much of the research into software for business customers was aimed at improving commonplace accounting routines, such as arranging data in tables or sorting it into numerical or alphabetical sequences. Hardware innovations centered principally around developing ancillary equipment such as faster, higher-capacity magnetic tape equipment for customers with outsized data files to handle.

No potential computer user fit that category more obviously than the U.S. Social Security Administration (the SSA), which had what was arguably the biggest bookkeeping job in the world. Since 1937, two years after the government-sponsored pension plan went into effect, the SSA's central recording offices in Baltimore had maintained records on the earnings of all working individuals in the country. The information was kept on standard punched cards. Each year, cards containing quarterly earnings reports and a summarized master record were created for every American worker. During the year, the cards were collated and updated. The cumulative data was then used to generate a new master card for the following year.

The only calculations required were those necessary to sort the cards according to social security number, to keep a running balance of each worker's account, and to figure the individual's benefits. But while the computations were relatively simple, the amount of data involved was staggering. By the mid-1950s the SSA was using more than 800 separate pieces of mechanical accounting equipment to manipulate 320 million cards annually. And that mind-boggling task was about to become much harder.

Amendments to the Social Security Act in 1954 required that after June 1956 the agency maintain a permanent record of each individual's yearly earnings as well as the cumulative total. The agency would now have to keep many more additional cards for each person. The SSA was in danger of drowning in an ocean of punched cards.

As early as 1945, Social Security data-processing experts had been studying electronic technology to see if the emerging science offered the agency a lifeline. But not until 1954, when IBM announced the 705—a follow-on machine to the 702, developed in part with an eye to the needs of the Social Security system—did the giant bureaucracy find a computer that could manage its workload.

The 705 was equipped to maintain huge volumes of data on a modest allotment of magnetic tape: The summary records of 60,000 individuals could fit on one 10½- inch reel. The system also included a new feature designed to expedite processing those records. This was a piece of hardware called a Tape Record Coordinator (TRC). The TRC had a limited amount of special memory called a buffer—a temporary reservoir for data—and a few special-purpose logic circuits, similar to those found in the main computer's CPU. The device shouldered some of the CPU's burden in managing tapes and transferring data by serving as an intermediary between the tapes and the CPU. Data in the buffer could be transferred into main memory much faster than data taken directly from tapes.

By the end of the decade the system had transformed data processing at the Social Security Administration. In one hour, the 705 could compute 20,000 claims—a job that had taken thirty-two hours on the old punch-card equipment. The agency's records had been packed into 6,250 cabinets spread over an area almost an acre in size; now the contents of each cabinet could be kept on a single reel of tape. In one operation alone—identifying and correcting erroneously reported earnings statements—the new equipment saved the SSA an estimated million dollars annually; the agency derived a much larger benefit from not having to hire the additional 800 employees that would have been needed to handle the extra work generated by the 1954 amendments. Such impressive savings in time, money, manpower, and floor space were in part a reflection of the sheer scale of the job. But they also testified to the efficiencies wrought by increasingly sophisticated components such as the TRC, a precursor of a far more complex and significant piece of hardware, called an input/output channel, introduced several years later on the IBM 709.

Channels were small special-purpose processors programmed with instructions that allowed them to independently store and retrieve data in the computer's memory. Thus, input/output operations could be conducted concurrently with the operations of the CPU, allowing the processor to work steadily at computations.

The input/output channel represented a major advance in computer technology and would soon become a feature of most large computers. It also led to a broader role for the computer operating system than that of a mere job scheduler. The intricate logistics of data movement between channel and computer—with pieces of data moving in and out of the machine at high speeds while the CPU was performing computations—demanded split-second control. To supply it, a special input/output control system (IOCS) was devised to synchronize the activities of the 709's CPU and its channels and was incorporated into the operating system designed for the computer. Thus the programmer did not have to worry about the complicated details of data movement; those activities were choreographed automatically and invisibly by the supervisory routines of the IOCS. Over the next decade, as computers continued to become faster, more powerful, and increasingly complex, the need for such software would only grow.

THE SECOND GENERATION

By the early 1960s, the manufacture of computers for commercial use was in full swing, and other companies had joined IBM and Sperry Rand (as Remington Rand had been renamed) in supplying the growing market. Among the most prominent were Burroughs, National Cash Register, Honeywell, RCA, Control Data Corporation, and General Electric. But it was IBM, later irreverently dubbed "Snow White" to the others' "Seven Dwarfs" by a waggish industry watcher, that dominated the scene with its thriving and loyal base of 700-series and 650 customers. With several years of computing experience behind them, these pioneering users were now primed for a second generation of IBM computers—machines that used transistors in their circuits, rather than the vacuum tubes that had been the building blocks of the first electronic computers.

The introduction of IBM's transistorized 7000 series, in the fall of 1958, marked the beginning of a new era in commercial data processing. A fraction the size of a tube, a transistor also consumed much less power, gave off less heat, and was many times more reliable—attributes it would pass on to the new computers. Each of IBM's established lines had transistorized successors. Flagship model of the 7000 series was the 7090, which replaced the line of scientific computers that had begun with the 701. Five times as fast as its vacuum-tube predecessor, it became the workhorse of scientific computing in the early 1960s. The business-oriented 705s were succeeded by the 7080, some six to ten times faster than the predecessors.

In 1959, IBM announced the moderately priced 1401, which was designed to appeal to 650 users and to small businesses that were still using mechanical punched-card machinery. The 1401, with its affordable base price (only $2,500 per month) and impressive performance (about seven times the speed of the old 650), became the most widely used computer of its day. Only about 6,000 general-purpose computers had been installed in the United States by the end of 1960; installations of the 1401 alone swiftly climbed to more than 15,000. It became the ubiquitous machine of office and industry in the early 1960s.

With the appearance of this robust second generation of IBM computers, and a varied tribe of competing machines from the smaller companies, computers assumed an ever-wider presence in society. In 1963 alone, U.S. businesses purchased or leased more than $4 billion worth of computer systems. The most

ardent single consumer of computing power was the federal government, which by 1963 was maintaining an electronic population of some 1,250 at agencies ranging from the Census Bureau to the Defense Department.

While the first generation of computers had carried out their chores almost unnoticed by the public at large, the second generation began to make their presence felt. "Big-Brother 7074 is Watching You," cautioned a *Popular Science* article, only half jokingly, in March 1963. The subject of the article was the new IRS computer facility at Martinsburg, which had just gone into action checking the 1962 tax returns filed by residents of the southeastern states.

At the heart of the operation was an IBM 7074 (an upgraded 7070) in Martinsburg, working in conjunction with a 1401 at the Atlanta Regional Service Center. In a tryout of the system that would ultimately be extended to the other tax centers, data from tax forms collected at the Atlanta office was fed into the 1401 on punched cards, checked for errors, then transferred to reels of magnetic tape. Flown to Martinsburg and loaded into the 7074, the magnetically coded returns were cross-checked with employers' wage reports and matched against master tapes containing individuals' permanent records to search for anomalies such as undeclared stock earnings.

So intimidating was the computer's reputation for accuracy that, shortly after the agency made its computerization plans public, fearful tax delinquents voluntarily turned in more than $700,000 in unpaid taxes. Over the next two years, as the two computers picked up errors and tax dodges that would otherwise have gone undetected, the IRS netted an extra $8.5 million in tax revenue from the southern region.

NEW OPERATING SYSTEMS

Computers like those at the IRS and at most other installations in the early 1960s were operated through batch processing. The desire for smooth running and efficient computing that had led to GM-NAA I/O and SOS in the mid-1950s had continued unabated into the age of transistors. Most computers, whether they were used for commercial or scientific applications, now ran under the control of some type of operating system, sometimes simply called a monitor or supervisor. On the whole, these systems were made up of routines designed to streamline the batch process by orchestrating the flow of work in and out of a computer so that the machine could be kept working continuously at or near peak capacity with a minimum of human intervention. A computer in an insurance company, for example, could move seamlessly from one job to the next, around the clock—from calculating premiums to processing claims, from preparing the staff payroll to updating the office inventory.

In addition to maintaining work flow, operating systems also automatically handled other computing resources—such as controlling printers or facilitating the use of high-level programming languages like FORTRAN or COBOL. To do the latter, the system was set up to recognize when a job was written in a given language and then to automatically invoke the appropriate conversion programs. Some operating systems included custom features that tailored computers for additional efficiencies. For example, a package of programs called the Direct Couple was appended to IBSYS, the operating system designed for IBM's 7090 computers. The Direct Couple software allowed a second, smaller computer (the IBM 7040) to act as an integrated peripheral processor for the larger machine, supervising the flow of information between the two and increasing machine-room efficiency.

Outside of IBM, other companies found even more innovative ways of increasing computer efficiency. One of the most radical was a technique called multiprogramming, introduced in 1961 by Burroughs for its 5000-series computers. Multiprogramming represented a sharp departure from the basic way computers had been used until that time. While processing had been speeded up considerably by various techniques designed to overlap CPU and input/output activity, a computer could still only work on one job at a time. Each job occupied main memory by itself and commanded the undivided attention of the CPU, which would have to complete all of the work on that job before turning to the next one. But with the Burroughs computer, under the supervision of an operating system called the Master Control Program (MCP), several users' jobs could share main memory at one time. The operating system assigned jobs to different memory locations and kept track of their whereabouts. It then scheduled computing time in such a way that the CPU always had part of a job ready to process. By shifting its attention rapidly among the jobs, processing small parts of each one in turn, the CPU could produce the results of more than one job at virtually the same instant.

Multiprogramming vastly increased a computer's ability to turn volumes of work around in a timely fashion. But it would take several years—and the introduction of a revolutionary new line of IBM computers—for multiprogramming to become widely adopted.

In 1964, IBM announced that the company would sweep aside all its existing computer products—which by then numbered seven separate and incompatible lines—and in their place provide a totally new and compatible single series of more advanced computers to meet the needs of scientists and businessmen alike. The machines were to be known collectively as System/360 for their ability to turn figuratively 360 degrees and be aimed at any application. To a large degree, the success or failure of the system would hinge on a revolutionary operating system, known simply as OS/360. As befitted the multibillion-dollar gamble that the computers represented, OS/360 was the most ambitious and expensive software-system package created up until that time. Between 1963 and 1966, IBM invested a staggering 5,000 man-years in the design, implementation, and documentation of this extraordinary body of software.

The result was the most comprehensive operating system developed to date. It incorporated all of the operating-system features created before—from input/output control systems to multiprogramming—and included the major features that would be part of operating systems from then on *(pages 25-37)*. OS/360 had commands for controlling all common peripheral devices and a set of routines to support each of the popular high-level programming languages. It was further augmented with special subsystems for specific applications—such as running projects for college students or handling large business data bases. Other parts of the operating system could manage the computer for interactive, on-line use, in which a user could carry on a kind of dialogue with the computer rather than sit back and wait for a batch program to run its course.

This everything-but-the-kitchen-sink approach produced an operating system of almost rococo complexity. It was criticized roundly by many computer experts, who pointed out that no one user would ever need more than a fraction of its numerous features. Nonetheless, OS/360 accomplished what it set out to do: give the 360 computer the flexibility to adapt itself to a broad spectrum of applications. Rather than relying on rigid software and hardware configurations developed by the manufacturers, computer buyers could now piece together equipment tailored to their own needs. Furthermore, they could update and alter those systems with relative ease.

The result was every bit as positive as IBM could have wished: System/ 360 was an enormous success in the marketplace. In 1966, two years after the system was announced, the company received one thousand orders a month for the new machines. Long-time IBM customers eagerly traded in their second generation computers for the more powerful and versatile 360s; some companies were so anxious to get their hands on a 360 that they bought places on IBM's waiting list from other firms. Several computer manufacturers—notably RCA and General Electric—were totally overwhelmed by the new competition and withdrew from the computer business entirely.

True to its promise, System/360 became a mainstay of businesses and universities, manufacturing and utility companies, and research laboratories. The federal government used it to set up and maintain central data bases containing libraries of scientific, engineering, and medical information. NASA used a pair of 360s to test the software aboard the Apollo spacecraft that carried men to the moon; at the Department of Transportation, the computer analyzed the traffic flow in American cities. In Japan, 360 components were at the heart of the world's first fully computerized newspaper system. The New York Stock Exchange employed a 360 audio unit in an automatic stock quotation service that could respond to telephone inquiries with digitally encoded oral replies. Another member of the 360 family monitored the entire electrical-generation and transmission network for the state of New York.

System/360 was a milestone in computer history, epitomizing the sophistication and versatility the machines had attained. Unlike their clumsy progenitors of the previous decade, computers were now clinically efficient machines. Capacious memory and backup storage, harnessed to streamlined CPUs and adept operating systems, gave computers an ability to manage, organize, and process information in a way that had never been possible before. And their allure only grew. From only a dozen or so computers at work in the United States in 1950, their numbers soared to more than 35,000 in 1966.

By then it was clear that computers were not only here to stay, but that they would have a profound effect on society as well. As John McCarthy, Professor of Computer Science at Stanford University, speculated in 1966: "The computer gives signs of becoming the contemporary counterpart of the steam engine that brought on the industrial revolution." Society was now in the grips of a new revolution—one that was still gathering momentum and whose true nature had yet to be seen.

Inside an Operating System

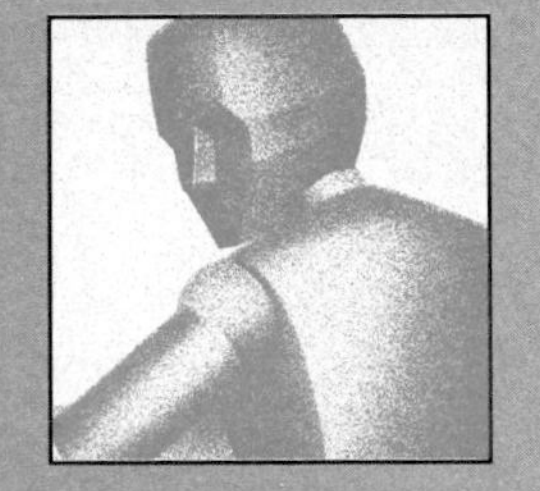

When a computer operator issues even the simplest command to the machine—calling up a word-processing program, for example—the computer responds by carrying out hundreds of electronic instructions at the rate of thousands or even millions of instructions per second: The computer accepts the name of the program through its input channels, searches long-term storage for the code, loads it into temporary memory, and displays the program's opening message on a video terminal.

The software that manages these essential functions comprises the machine's operating system, an enormous complex that, in the case of a mainframe computer, may contain millions of instructions. Yet it is the very complexity of this software that simplifies the work of users and makes possible the sweeping variety of tasks assigned to these machines in a computerized society.

Programmers and engineers have designed many different types of operating systems. Some, like the process-control systems that run computers dedicated to the management of oil refining, manufacturing, and other industries, are only marginally concerned with human users. Others serve individuals. Multiuser systems, which allow many people simultaneous access to a computer, are perhaps the most versatile. These systems juggle incoming and outgoing streams of data so smoothly that anyone working with the machine has the illusion of exclusive access to all its vast resources.

A wide variety of multiuser operating systems are available. File-interrogation systems permit access to massive data bases, repositories for medical records, library holdings, financial data, and many other kinds of information that changes relatively infrequently—once a day, perhaps. Transaction-processing systems handle never-static data bases such as those used to book airplane seats. And general-purpose operating systems allow many people to work concurrently at a variety of tasks on a single computer.

Most operating systems are organized into groups of programs, represented on the following pages by a series of managerial figures. Together, the managers assure a smoothly operating computer by carrying out their own responsibilities flawlessly and by closely coordinating their activities with those of their electronic peers.

Introducing the Management Team

The figures in the limelight at right are the managers in a general-purpose, multiuser operating system. Most such operating [illegible]ystems permit the computer to function in two ways: batch or interactive. In batch processing—calculating a company payroll, for example—the computer receives data and a [illegible] processing commands, which are executed without [illegible]log between computer and user until the job is comp[illegible]. In the interactive mode, employed for word processing [illegible]nd other tasks that require immediate response from the computer, the operating system acknowledges each command as it is issued through one of the multitude of terminals connected to the machine.

Pe[illegible]e interact with the computer through the controller, seated [illegible]t the front desk. Every batch job and each command issued [illegible]rough an interactive program crosses the controller's desk en route to one or more of four managers, each of whom super[illegible]es an essential area of operation: the computer's input/[illegible]put (I/O) functions; sending files to external storage device[illegible]nd retrieving them; allocating space in the computer's [illegible]ternal memory; and regulating the central processing unit (CPU). Together, the controller and managers see that each user gets a share of the machine's computing power. To coordinate their efforts, the controller and managers keep record[illegible] their activities and communicate with each other by me[illegible] of signals such as semaphores *(pages 42-43)* and throug[illegible]perating-system mailboxes—areas reserved in the comp[illegible] memory for messages among the managers and betwee[illegible]hem and the controller.

On the following pages, a visit inside the computer to the "office" occupied by each manager reveals the role each plays in processing a single interactive command, or job—for exam[illegible]playing a letter typed at the keyboard on a termina[illegible] a file from storage, or printing a document. The controller divides the job, colored blue to distinguish it from the ot[illegible]bs *(silver)* that the computer must also accommoda[illegible]o component operating-system tasks—recording keystro[illegible]in an area of memory called a buffer, for instance, or searching memory for data and programs, or routing a byte to the CPU. Assisted by the managers, the controller also keeps track of each task as it zips around the computer.

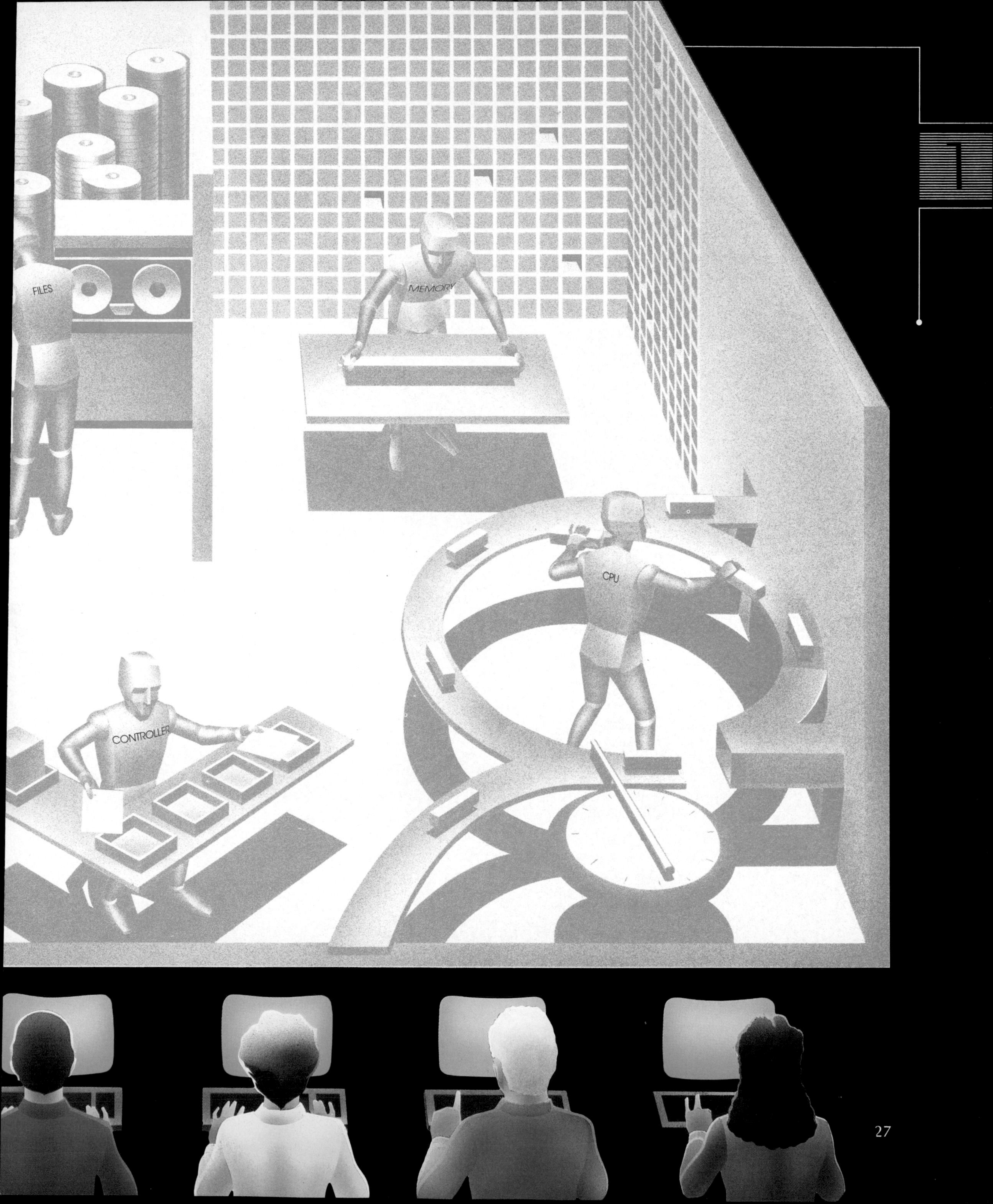
FILES
MEMORY
CPU
CONTROLLER
1

The Controller

At the figurative center of an operating system is the controller. Every request for computer services, whether it comes in the form of an entire set of instructions for a batch job or a single command in an interactive job, is issued in language understandable to the controller, who examines each item in turn to determine which of the computer's resources it requires. The controller then passes the information to the appropriate resource managers.

As part of the review of in-box contents on the desk of his imaginary office, the controller logs in each job, then divides each one into component tasks for the managers to process. Each task receives a descriptor, a code that tells the controller and the CPU manager where to look in the computer's memory for information about the status of the task—whether it has been completed or what remains unfinished—as the system executes it step by step. Updated constantly, these status reports permit the controller and the managers to make moment-to-moment decisions about which piece of which job should be processed next. This information also allows the CPU manager to suspend processing in the middle of a task *(pages 36-37)*, then to resume processing later without missing or repeating a step.

Besides managing the flow of work through a computer, the controller may have the additional duty of guarding the system against unauthorized use. In the role of security monitor, the controller checks an individual's request for computer services against electronic access lists. At the very least, the controller confirms by password that a person has been granted computer privileges. In many systems, additional checks establish whether users, after being allowed into the computer, have permission to use the computer as they wish.

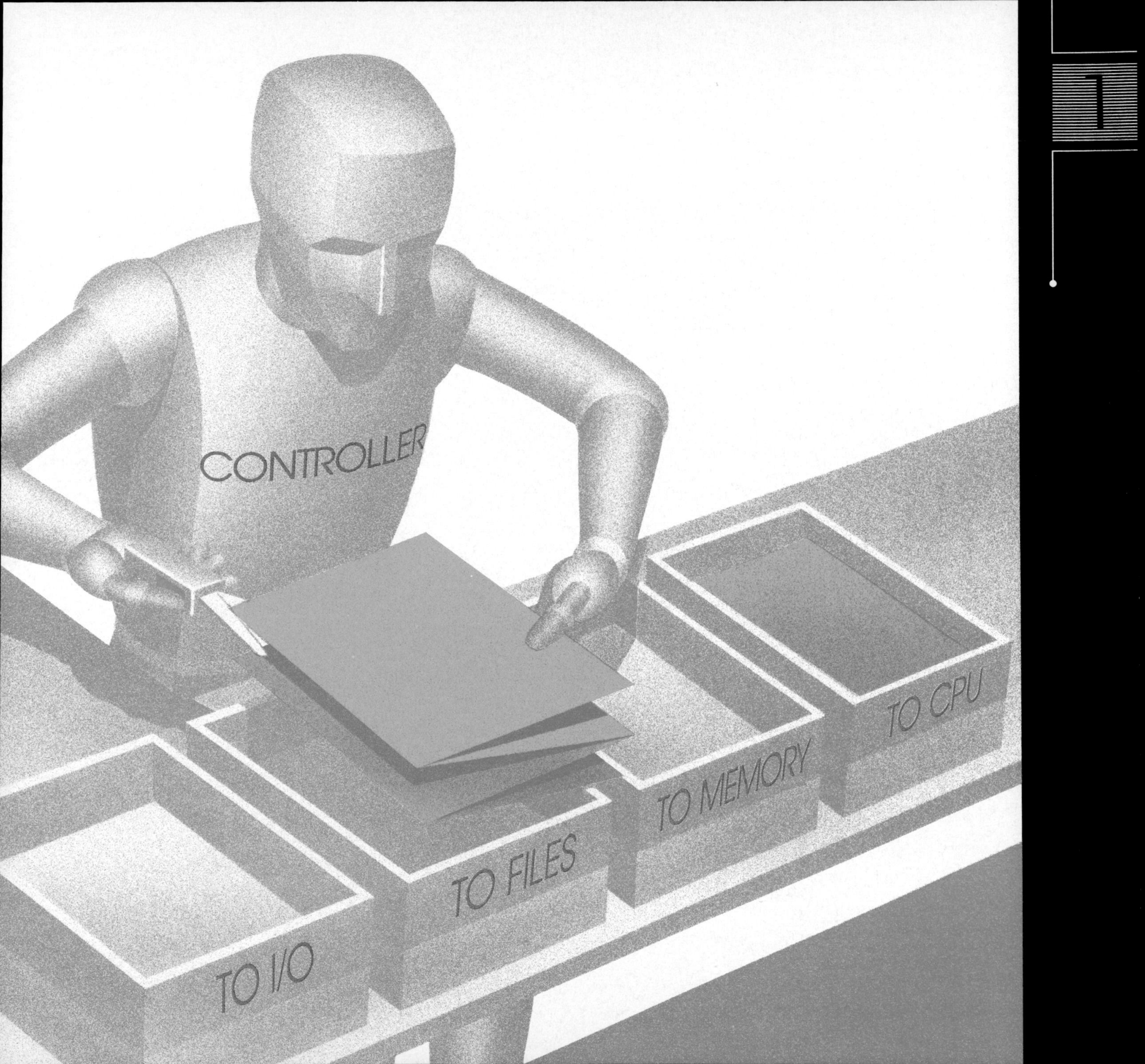
CONTROLLER
TO I/O
TO FILES
TO MEMORY
TO CPU

The Input/Output Manager

Pictured here as the operator of an intricate switchboard, the input/output manager is responsible for some of the computer's most crucial procedures. Indeed, the earliest operating systems were nothing more than programs that handled I/O functions without which computers and their human taskmasters could not communicate. The I/O manager coordinates the computer's interaction with many input and output devices at the same time. In addition, the I/O manager must accommodate differences in speed between the CPU, which can process tens of millions of bits per second, and devices such as keyboards and graphics plotters, which may send out or accept as few as several hundred bits per second. To prevent the system from being hobbled by these enormous inequalities, the manager uses buffers in memory as temporary storage for data waiting its turn for processing in the CPU. In addition, the I/O manager is responsible for directing traffic to and from shareable hardware—devices such as disk drives that can deal with several tasks simultaneously—and others such as printers that must concentrate on one assignment at a time. To deal with long waits for unshareable devices, the manager can use a technique known as spooling, holding large amounts of data temporarily on a disk or other storage medium until the necessary equipment becomes free.

Keeping track of all the jobs moving in and out of the computer requires the I/O manager to store in memory information on the system's input and output resources. Updated continuously, this data offers the manager an instant status report to determine which input and output devices are available for assignments. If one or more tasks require an I/O device that is temporarily busy, the manager creates a queue, lining up the I/O requests according to priority in some systems, or on a first-come, first-served basis in others. Amid this flurry of activity, the I/O manager must also keep in touch with other managers in the operating system. He uses signals called interrupts to notify the CPU manager when the I/O portion of one task is finished or when another is ready to be processed. For information on the whereabouts of data in the computer's storage, he consults the file manager.

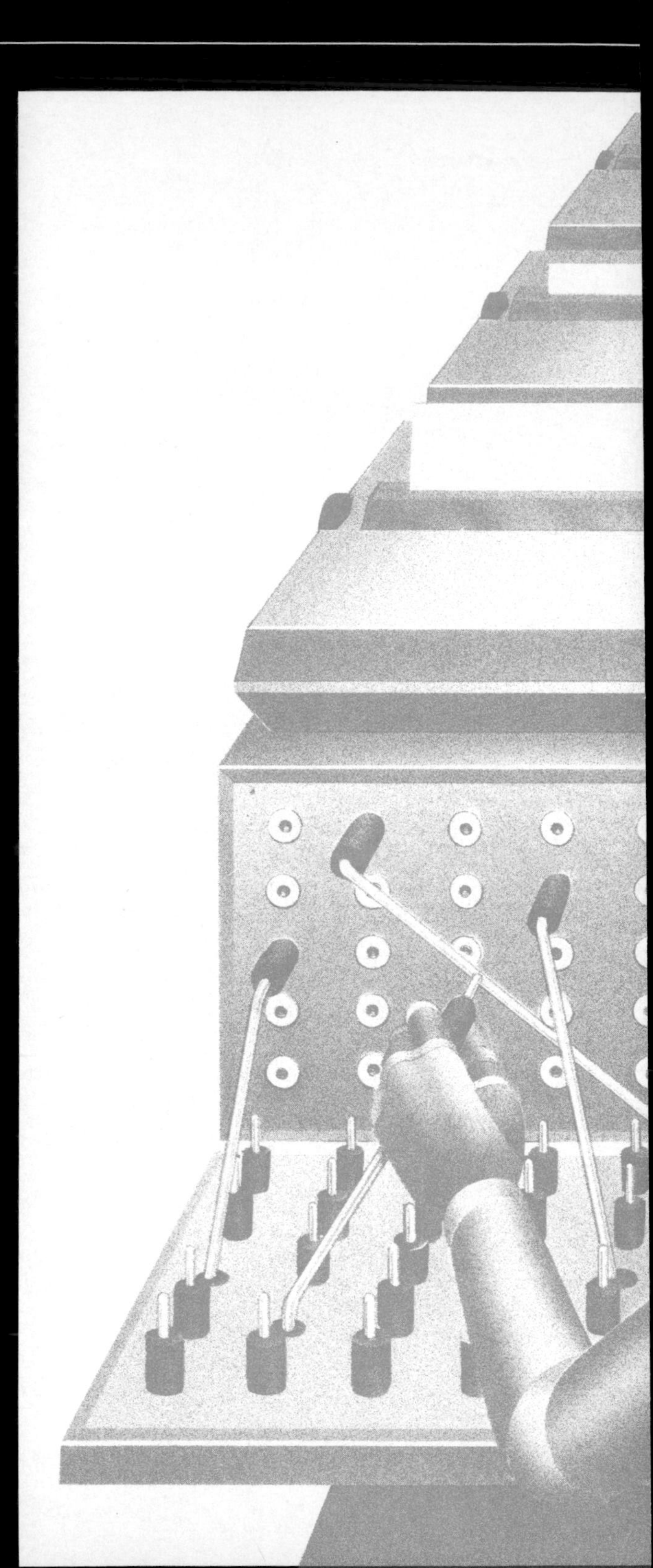

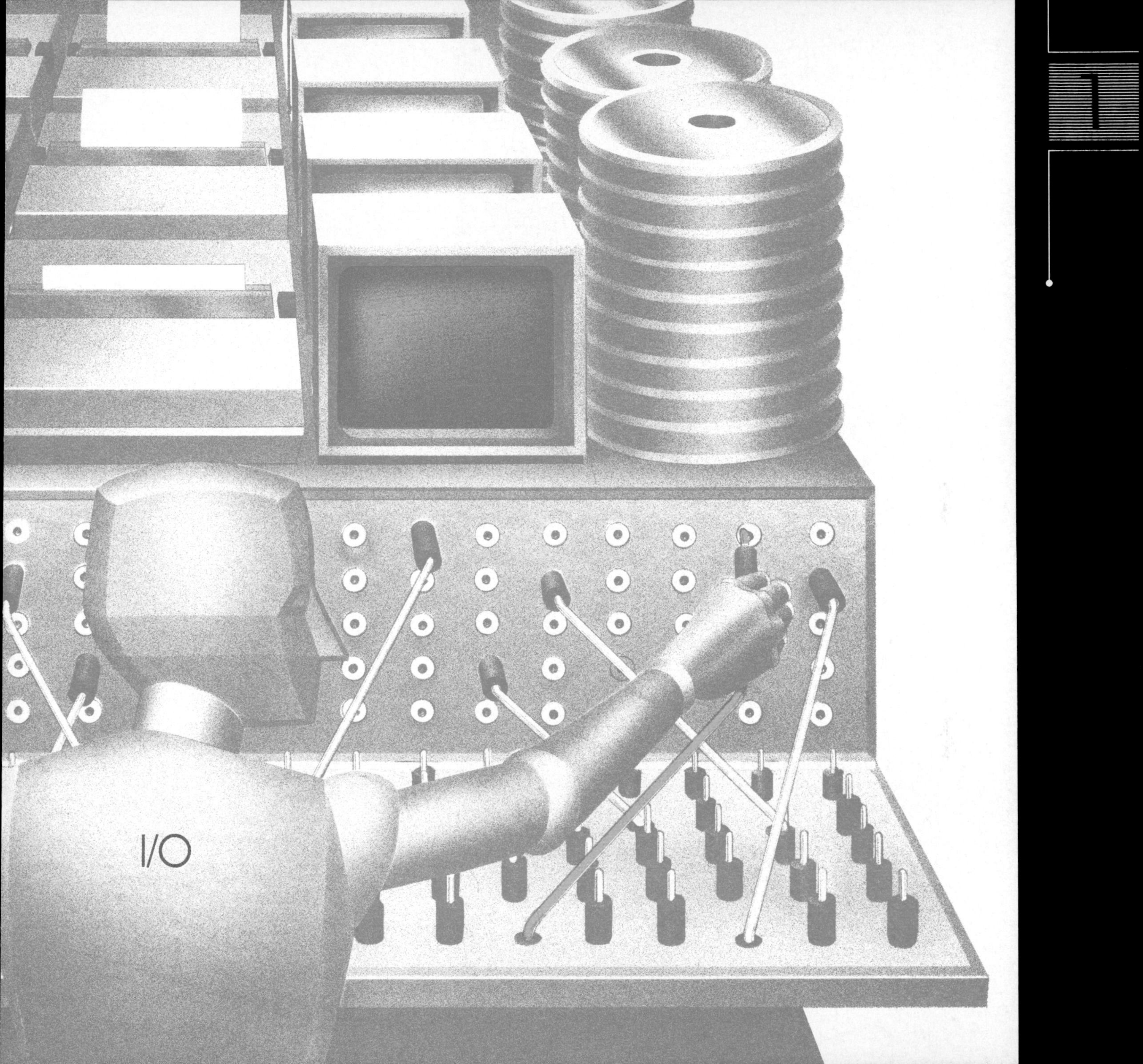
I/O

The File Manager

In the course of virtually any computer job, many requests are made to locate programs and data in the computer's long-term, external storage. The operating system's file manager performs these duties and others. He is responsible for finding space to keep new files and for deleting old files when asked to do so. In addition, the file manager limits access to stored information to those authorized to see it.

The key to success in keeping tabs on thousands of files is knowing precisely where each one resides. The file manager accomplishes this by maintaining a master directory of storage contents, updating it whenever a new file is created or an old file modified or erased. When data is stored on tape, all the bits in a file are kept together in sequence.

With disk storage, however, a file can be widely scattered among disk packs, as shown here. It is the file manager's responsibility to find the pieces when asked to do so. This storage strategy may seem haphazard, but it conserves storage space by allowing the file manager to fill any size vacancy by splitting long files into small pieces.

To help the file manager handle this complexity, each section of a file ends with a pointer, a notation indicating where the next segment of the file is stored. Kept in a directory, pointers to the first segment of each file allow the file manager quickly and unerringly to reassemble file components wherever they may reside.

Whether information is stored on tape or on disk, the name of the file, accompanied by the appropriate command issued to the operating system's controller from a computer terminal, begins the process that calls the data from storage. The controller passes the name to the file manager, who then consults the master list to assemble the appropriate response. Once the file manager has located the requested information, he calls on the I/O manager to convey it to its destination, which might be a terminal, a printer, or a modem, the device that connects a computer to the telephone network.

FILES

The Memory Manager

Each task of a job requires space in the computer's short-term, electronic memory before it can be processed. It is the duty of the memory manager to determine how much memory a task needs and to supervise the allocation to assure that a task is not assigned to space that is already occupied.

The operating system's memory manager is shown here taking the measure of a task that has just arrived from the controller by way of the I/O manager. Behind him is the computer's memory, represented as cubbyholes. In this machine, memory is divided into sections of equal size called pages. Depending on the computer and the operating system, a page can hold as many as several thousand bytes of data. The memory manager divides a task into page-length sections and assigns each one to an empty cubbyhole. As is the case with disk storage, components of a task may be widely scattered in memory.

If all the cubbyholes are full—as is usually the case in a busy computer system—the memory manager takes advantage of an operating-system feature called virtual memory to make room for the new arrival. When additional space is needed for data or programs, the memory manager uses the task status reports prepared by the controller to identify memory pages that are occupied by tasks that need not reside in memory at the moment; he shifts those tasks to storage and fills the cubbyholes with new data or programs. If the former contents are needed, they are quickly returned to memory from storage, displacing idle information as necessary.

One of the few items never to be shifted out of memory to storage is a reference table that serves as a guide to the location of each page in memory. Thanks to this table, updated instant by instant, the memory manager is always able to find all the pieces of every task.

MEMORY

The CPU Manager

Every job that enters the operating system seeks immediate access to the computing power of the CPU. Operating-system tasks required to manage the computer itself also compete for the CPU's attention. The critical function of the CPU manager is to schedule this work in an efficient manner. Shown here organizing a queue of tasks for processing, the CPU manager has interspersed blue-job tasks with tasks from other jobs so that each receives a share of CPU time.

Under the "time slice" scheduling method used by this operating system, the task at the head of the queue enters the CPU for a fixed period—perhaps 300 milliseconds—represented by a single sweep of a timer. If the task is finished at the end of a time slice, the CPU sends the results to the memory manager for temporary storage, and the next task enters the CPU for its slice of processing time. Unfinished tasks are returned to the queue to await another turn.

The CPU manager has several options for setting priorities. Each time a new task enters the queue, the CPU manager can revise his priorities and rearrange the waiting tasks accordingly. A task can jump immediately to the head of the line if the manager decides—judging from current demands on the CPU and past experience with the task itself—that doing so is the most efficient way to proceed. For example, the CPU manager might wish to start a task that needs several slices of time in the CPU ahead of shorter tasks, so that no task is unduly delayed.

In certain cases, the manager allows a task with especially high priority—typically, an operating-system task related to I/O operations or an indication of a system malfunction—to bump another task from the CPU in the middle of its time slice. The red task shown cutting in at the head of the line was activated in response to an operating-system signal known as an interrupt—so-named because it alerts the CPU manager to momentarily suspend one computer operation in favor of another. To respond to the interrupt, the CPU first performs a step known as context switching, which makes a precise record of the contents in the CPU. The contents, representing a partially processed task, are then stored in a holding area called an interrupt stack. After dealing with the higher priority task, the CPU then recalls the unfinished work from the stack and resumes processing.

It is possible for a task that caused an interrupt to be interrupted in turn by work with even higher priority. When that happens, another context switch takes place and the second interrupted task is stacked on top of the first. When the CPU resumes processing tasks from the interrupt stack, the last task to be stacked is always the first to be recalled.

CPU

The Responsive Machine

2

Twenty-four hours a day, 365 days a year, the "911" emergency calls from New York City's five boroughs come in to the police department's communications headquarters in lower Manhattan. An armed robbery in Brooklyn. An apartment fire in Queens. A heart attack on a street in Staten Island. A man threatening to jump from a window ledge in the Bronx. Almost all the calls are answered within thirty seconds. Once received, they are screened and analyzed, and a patrol car is dispatched. Five minutes after a citizen dials 911, police can be at the scene—an extraordinary response time, considering that New York's 911 system handles 18,000 calls a day, or well over six million a year.

A computer system called SPRINT (for Special Police Radio Inquiry Network) enables New York's finest to cope with this deluge of appeals for help. SPRINT is part of a complex data and communications network linking automobile and foot patrols, ambulance and helicopter units, and the fire department. At its heart is an IBM computer that uses a specialized operating system called an ACP (for Airline Control Program, because it was originally developed as a reservation system for airlines). The ACP manages a vast amount of information stored in the computer's memory and makes it instantly available to the hundreds of operators and dispatchers on duty—information that includes a complete map of New York City and the location of police and emergency resources available at any given time.

SPRINT is an example of what is known as on-line transaction processing, or OLTP. In computer terms, a transaction is the exchange of a piece of information between the machine and a user. In the case of the 911 system, for example, the operator enters the street address where a burglary has been committed, and the computer responds by displaying the numbered sector of the city where the address lies. Because the operator taps directly into the computer, the transaction is said to occur on-line.

In the broadest sense, the term on-line refers to any type of computer use in which a person has immediate, continuous access to the machine's central processing unit (CPU) and its main memory throughout a computing job. On-line processing differs fundamentally from batch processing, in which the user relinquishes control of a job once it is delivered to the computer and has to wait until the job is completed before receiving the results. In practical terms, this usually means waiting at least several hours—typically overnight—because of the way work is scheduled in most batch processing computer installations. With on-line processing, on the other hand, results are available at once.

Transaction processing is an on-line technique introduced in the early 1960s to allow computer users to quickly retrieve information stored in a computer data base, alter it, and add new information. A key characteristic of an OLTP system is its ability to service many users at once. Large national and international on-line networks may link thousands of remote terminals to a single mainframe computer and the contents of its data base. At any moment, hundreds of people may be interacting with the computer simultaneously. Thanks to a deft operating system designed for the job, the computer juggles these transactions with such speed and efficiency that each person is left with the illusion that he or she alone is communicating with the machine.

The advent of OLTP democratized the computer world. With batch processing as the principal mode of operation (as it was well into the 1960s), the primary value of computers had been as supercalculators that could crunch numbers and process large volumes of data at high speeds. Computers were isolated from the workaday world and operated only by highly trained professionals. Transaction processing, by contrast, is used chiefly to keep track of large volumes of constantly changing information. OLTP put computer terminals on the desks of travel agents, salesclerks and bank tellers, all of whom became computer users simply by learning a few commands.

On-line transaction processing has become so much a part of the routine of life as to be taken entirely for granted. It is, in fact, a little bit like oxygen: invisible but essential. With on-line transaction systems, airline and hotel clerks, travel and car-rental agents make immediate reservations anywhere in the world. Store clerks "go on-line" when dialing into a central computer to check credit cards. Increasingly, companies are turning to such systems to control inventory and as a guide for setting prices; with the appropriate software, for example, a retailer can track the day-to-day movement of merchandise and gauge the optimum time to put something on sale. An on-line system tailored to the needs of a manufacturer can save millions of dollars in warehousing costs by precisely controlling the supply of parts.

The result has been nothing less than a quantum leap in corporate efficiency. The ability to find and change information almost instantaneously has enabled companies to provide faster, more flexible, and more complete service to their customers and to manage their resources much more adroitly.

A PIONEERING SYSTEM FOR AIRLINES

The first commercial on-line transaction system to come into widespread use grew out of a chance meeting in the spring of 1953, when R. Blair Smith, a senior salesman for IBM, boarded a transcontinental flight in Los Angeles and sat down beside C. R. Smith, the president of American Airlines. The two executives soon began talking about American's need for an automated system for booking reservations—at the time largely a manual process. Air travel was burgeoning, and reservation clerks were hard pressed to keep pace. The encounter eventually led to an eight-year collaboration between IBM and American Airlines that resulted in SABRE, a computerized reservation system that transformed the airline industry when it was finally introduced in 1964.

SABRE (an acronym for Semi-Automated Business Research Environment) was an enormous information engine built around a pair of IBM 7090 mainframe computers that were located in Briarcliff Manor, 30 miles north of New York City. The two computers, one serving as backup to the other in case of a breakdown, were linked by telephone lines to about 2,000 reservation clerks around the country. Each clerk could tap into a common data base—a pool of information about all of American's flights and passengers—and instantly check on the availability of space on any flight, reserve a seat, and update the inventory by eliminating the newly assigned seat from the number available.

At the core of the system was ACP, the Airline Control Program developed by IBM to manage SABRE. ACP was a specialized operating system containing two key features—groups of programs, actually—that would be employed in all other on-line transaction processing systems in the future: a transaction monitor and a data-base manager. The transaction monitor served as the chief resource manager and telecommunications director, with the crucial function of shuttling transactions in and out of the computer for processing. The data-base manager kept track of the seat and passenger inventory, which was recorded on sixteen magnetic disk storage units.

Soon American's 2,000 reservation clerks were making 85,000 calls daily to Briarcliff Manor, communicating via teletypewriters (later replaced with video display terminals). The act of making a reservation—asking the computer for the seat status of a particular flight, reserving a seat, and reducing the seat inventory by one—took at least three transactions (and often several more) to complete. Each transaction began with what was essentially a request for time on the computer's central processing unit. As the request came into the computer, the transaction monitor placed it in a queue. When that request's turn came, the transaction monitor passed it on to the CPU, which began processing the transaction by instructing the data-base manager to locate in the data base the necessary information (for example, the number of seats still available on a given flight), fetch it from the disk, and bring it into the computer's main memory. The applications program continued processing the transaction by manipulating the data in some fashion and finally signaling the transaction monitor to send the information back over the phone line to the waiting clerk, thus completing the transaction.

At peak hours, with many clerks reserving seats at the same time, the ACP had to organize hundreds of such transactions within minutes. Although the CPU could execute only one transaction at a time, it worked so fast—spending a total of perhaps two seconds on each—that the computer seemed to be processing many transactions at once. This electronic sleight-of-hand was an example of what is called concurrent processing.

The relationship between users and the computer in concurrent processing has been likened to that between customers in a diner and the diner's short-order cook. Although the cook may be working on several orders at once, he is never doing more than one thing at a time—cracking eggs on the griddle, for instance, then flipping a hamburger, then popping bread into a toaster. As the orders are completed and delivered, each customer has the impression that the cook has worked on his order exclusively.

ACP, the digital maestro responsible for choreographing this activity for SABRE, was soon in demand by other airlines. IBM built two other ACP-based reservation systems, called Deltamatic and PANAMAC, for Delta and Pan American airlines respectively. Like SABRE, they ran on the IBM 7000 series mainframe. In 1965, IBM also began to develop a generic reservation system to run on its new 360 computer. Known as PARS (Program Airline Reservation System), the new product was introduced in 1968. It registered an instant success—particularly among smaller airlines, which could not afford the start-up costs of a custom system like SABRE, even though by this time the price of computers

Stop on 0, Go on 1

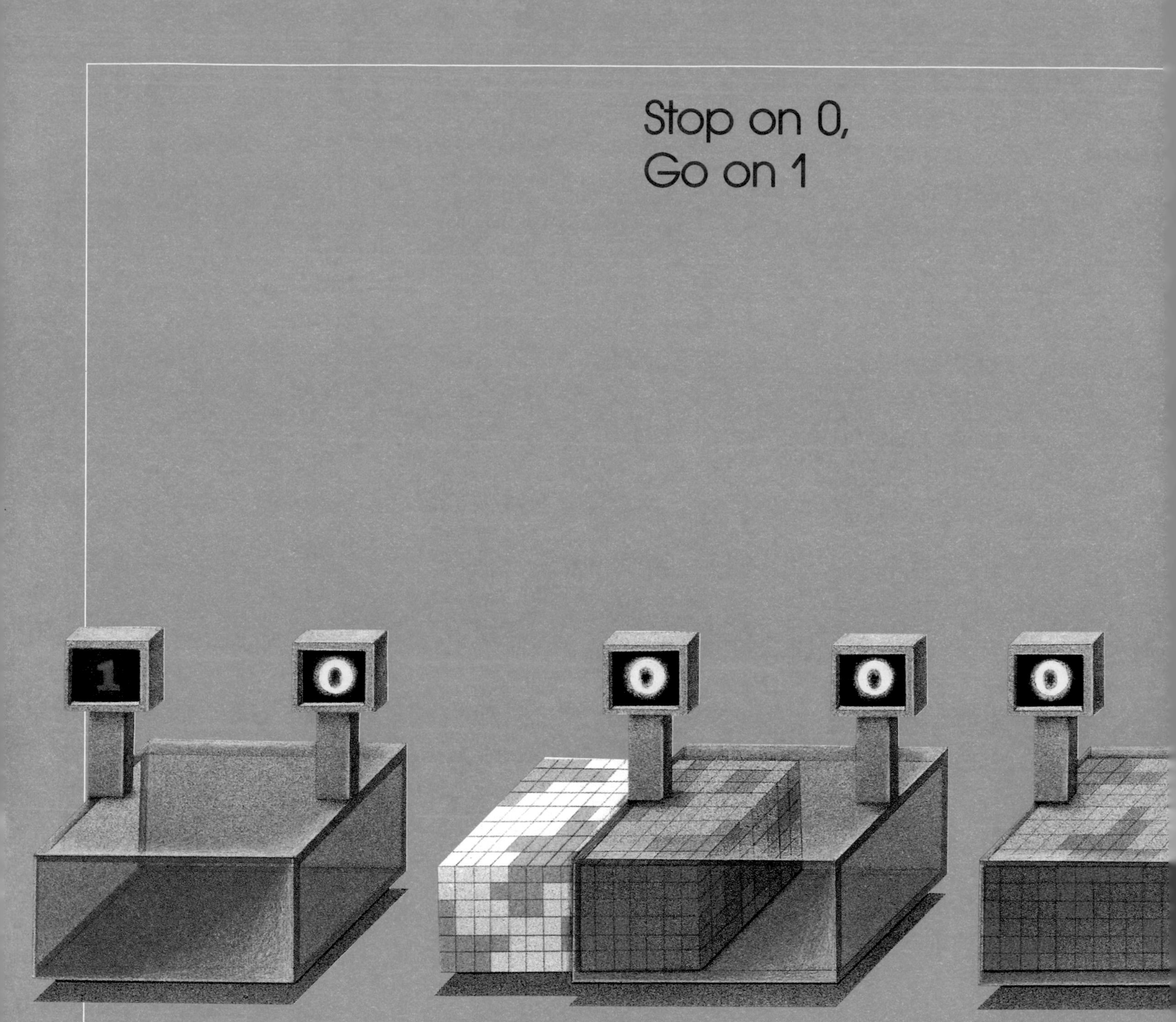

An empty buffer *(clear box)* signals its status with two semaphores—one aimed at tasks that would load data into the buffer, the other at those that would unload data from it. The left-hand semaphore is initially set to 1 to indicate that the buffer is available for filling; the right-hand 0 means there is not yet any data to be unloaded.

Having detected the "available" signal, a data-loading task first changes the left-hand semaphore to 0, which keeps any other tasks from interfering by informing them that the buffer is now in use; the original task then begins feeding in a buffer-size chunk of data *(block of cubes)*.

When the buffer is full, the loading task switches the right-hand semaphore to 1, signaling that data is now available for unloading.

In the busy environs of an operating system *(pages 24-37)*, multiple tasks often compete for a computer's resources—data and program files, printers and plotters, chunks of memory. To keep activities from interfering with one another in a chaotic scramble for the limited supply of these commodities, operating systems employ semaphores to let each task know the availability of any resource at every moment.

A semaphore is a one-bit signpost in memory that a task checks before attempting to use a given asset. A 0 signifies that the resource is in use; a 1 indicates that it is unoccupied. Coming upon a 0 semaphore, a task waits until the sign shows a 1. To proceed, the task immediately changes the semaphore to 0, denying the resource to other operations. Upon finishing its business, the task rewrites a 1 on the signpost, clearing the way for the next operation. In this manner, each task gets exclusive, uninterrupted use of any computer asset it needs.

When the resource is a device such as a printer, which handles each job independently, a lone semaphore suffices to control access and eliminate confusion. But sometimes two or more tasks must use a single resource in a coordinated fashion, a situation that requires more complex signaling.

In the example below, a pair of semaphores is needed to regulate the flow of activity through a buffer, an area of memory used in the transfer of data to a storage disk. Because of the division of labors imposed by the operating system, one task takes care of loading data into the buffer, while another task sees to removing the data and passing it on.

Without two different semaphores, the process would quickly go awry: The second task might try to remove data before it was available, or the first task could accidentally write over data before it had been removed from the buffer. But as the sequence below illustrates, with two separate semaphores keeping each task in line, the transfer proceeds without a hitch.

Alerted to the presence of data by the right-hand semaphore, the unloading task starts emptying the buffer, but only after changing the right-hand semaphore back to 0 so that no other unloading tasks will try to gain access to the resource.

After all the data has been removed from the buffer, the unloading task switches the left-hand semaphore back to 1, thereby signaling to the loading task that space is once more available. The entire sequence can then be repeated to transfer more data.

was rapidly coming down. A related system named IPARS was soon marketed to international air carriers. In all, by the 1980s, more than twenty carriers would purchase IBM reservation systems based on ACP technology.

COMPUTER UTILITIES

At about the same time that ACP began to transform the airline industry, another concurrent on-line computing technique was developed, and it appeared to hold equally great commercial promise. Called time-sharing, it grew out of the need of scientists at universities to make efficient use of their campus mainframes. Like OLTP, time-sharing was an interactive system that gave a computer user instant results, eliminating the frustration of waiting overnight or longer for a batch job to be completed. A scientist working on a mathematical description of a complex chemical reaction, for example, could use on-line capability to spot flaws in a formula and fix them immediately. On a long project, the time thus saved could add up to weeks or months.

The root of time-sharing as a practical concept was an influential memo drafted in 1959 by John McCarthy, a professor of communications sciences, and sent to his colleagues at the Massachusetts Institute of Technology. The memo called for a radically new operating system that would "substantially reduce the time required to get a problem solved on the machine." McCarthy's initiative led to the development of CTSS (for Compatible Time-Sharing System, because it was compatible with any program that ran on M.I.T.'s IBM 709 computer). The constellation of programs that made up CTSS was introduced in the year 1961. As the first operational time-sharing system, CTSS became a milestone in the history of computers.

The crucial element of the CTSS operating system was a group of routines called the "executive" or "supervisor." Roughly analogous to the ACP's transaction monitor, the supervisor coordinated the operation of the system components, controlled access to the system and—most important—parceled out time on the CPU to each user. An internal clock enabled the supervisor to divide CPU time into razor-thin slices that were measured in milliseconds and were meted out to users in a round-robin sequence. The supervisor software also included a scheduling program for assigning priorities to users according to the length of time required to complete a project.

CTSS bore obvious similarities to ACP. Both were interactive, multiuser operating systems that did concurrent processing, giving each of many users the impression of having exclusive access to a computer. But the two systems varied fundamentally in purpose, and not surprisingly, they came to be used for very different applications. The Airline Control Program was designed in such a way that the computer it operated could serve only a single, limited purpose; every user on the system had access to the same data. By contrast, CTSS was devised so that the computer could be put to work solving all sorts of problems, employing whatever programs were needed. Users had access only to the data stored in their individual files. There was no common data base; indeed, the time-sharing operating system was deliberately designed to prevent unauthorized sharing of files so that one user could not inadvertently (or maliciously) interfere with another's work.

While originally developed to give scientists and academics convenient access to computers, time-sharing soon attracted the attention of businessmen. They saw it as a practical way to put computer power in the hands of organizations whose needs or means were limited.

By the mid-1960s, a number of time-sharing services were offering computer time as a commercial product. Keydata Corporation of Cambridge, Massachusetts, provided on-line accounting and inventory control for small manufacturers and wholesale firms. Another Massachusetts firm known as MEDINET provided hospitals with a comprehensive software package that enabled them to share time on a mainframe; among its many functions, a MEDINET system could be used to find an empty bed for a new patient, instruct a ward nurse what medications to give, and make up an outgoing patient's bill. The clients of a California company called Tymeshare shared two Scientific Data Systems 940 computers, one located near San Francisco and the other in Los Angeles. Typical Tymeshare customers were large scientific and engineering firms, some of whom already owned computers that were programmed exclusively for big number-intensive batch-processing jobs. They turned to Tymeshare for smaller jobs requiring quick answers.

By the late 1960s, such centralized computer "utilities," providing computing services in the manner of telephone or power companies, had fostered the creation of a whole new group of computer users. But in the 1970s, commercial time-sharing began to wane. At about that time, integrated circuits began to take the place of transistors as the computer's switching element, a change that vastly increased the power of computers while at the same time reducing their cost. As the price of hardware dropped, organizations that had relied on time-sharing networks for their computing needs bought their own computers. And many businesses began to explore the benefits of on-line transaction processing. As a mode of computing specifically designed to keep track of large volumes of constantly changing data, OLTP was inherently better suited to the requirements of consumer-oriented companies.

ORGANIZING A SPACE PROBE

International Business Machines, the behemoth of the computer industry, had uncharacteristically taken a back seat to other manufacturers in time-sharing. Internal conflicts between IBM's marketing and technological people had hampered the design of its major time-sharing system, known as TSS, which reached the market several years behind schedule and lost millions of dollars. IBM had far better luck with transaction processing. At the same time that the company was selling ACP-based reservation systems to the airlines, other customers began asking for on-line systems.

One such customer was North American Rockwell, a giant aerospace company that in 1961 was chosen by the U.S. Government as prime contractor for the Apollo spacecraft, destined to take the first men to the moon. The job eventually involved working with a staggering inventory of two million parts and thousands of engineering drawings scattered among numerous locations at Rockwell's space division plant in Downey, California. Nor could North American Rockwell limit its attention to its internal operations: The Apollo effort was worldwide in scope, and requests for information on the status of the project and its myriad components could originate almost anywhere on the globe.

To handle the challenge, a joint team of Rockwell and IBM personnel in 1965 began to devise an on-line inventory system that would run on the aerospace company's IBM 7010. In concept it was similar to the Airline Control Program. It consisted of a data-base manager to keep track of information on the whereabouts of parts or drawings and a transaction monitor to juggle requests from users—in this case engineers who were trying to locate a part or put their hands on a particular design specification.

When Rockwell decided to replace its 7010 with one of the powerful new IBM 360s, the two companies set about reworking the inventory—tracking software and making it more general in function. But it soon became clear that the partners were on divergent paths. As a key team member later wrote: "IBM wanted to develop a marketable product. Rockwell wanted to go to the moon."

In 1967 Rockwell dissolved its working relationship with IBM on the project (initially called ICS, for Information Control System, but later renamed IMS, for Information Management System). In negotiating the divorce, Rockwell agreed to redesign its transaction monitor/data-base manager as a subsystem for the 360's operating system, designated OS-360. In return, IBM would maintain the software, altering it as needed so that it would remain compatible with the 360 computer as improvements in the machine and its operating system came along. In the view of at least one member of the Rockwell team, "IBM had struck the greatest bargain since the Dutch bought Manhattan from the Indians."

IMS went into action on Rockwell's 360 computer in 1968, working as what was called a batch-applications program in a "top priority partition." This meant that while the 360 computer was batch processing (it spent most of its working day running engineering calculations), the IMS transaction monitor was on standby in a separate section of the computer's memory. Whenever an engineer or plant worker stepped up to one of the terminals located around the assembly plant to type in a request for information, the request was conveyed over in-plant telephone lines. On receiving the call, the transaction monitor figuratively tapped the 360's operating system on the shoulder, making it interrupt batch processing and turn the CPU over to IMS long enough to process the transaction and send a reply to the waiting worker. At least in part because of IMS, a project that could easily have become mired in chaos produced one of the great engineering triumphs of the century, the craft that touched down on the moon with three Americans aboard in 1969.

At about the time that IMS was being developed in California, IBM was working on a similar on-line system in collaboration with a big Chicago-area utility company, Commonwealth Edison. The utility wanted an on-line, interactive system that its service representatives could use, for example, when fielding an inquiry by a homeowner about last month's electricity bill or when changing a customer's mailing address. From a computing standpoint, an OLTP system was the only feasible way to deal with the large number of users (more than 200 service representatives taking phone calls during business hours) and the company's large central data base, which held facts about the utility's 2.5 million customers.

Together, Commonwealth Edison and IBM went to work on a Customer Information System, or CIS, for the IBM 360 computer the utility had just ordered. Writing and debugging the software was to take the better part of four years, but when CIS was unveiled in 1968, Commonwealth Edison could boast the nation's first on-line real-time service for utility customers. Although the kind of service CIS provided is routine today, its effect was astonishing then. Customers telephoning for information about their accounts, for example, were startled when service representatives called them by name after the customers had given only their addresses. More important, the callers could get instant answers to questions about their bills, almost as though the service representative were there in the room and looking over the bill with them.

In March of 1968, IBM announced a commercial version of its Information Management System and was flooded by orders from manufacturers, large retail stores, and other firms that wanted to add an on-line inventory-control capability similar to Rockwell's to the 360 computers they used for batch jobs such as billing. In similar fashion, IBM adapted Commonwealth Edison's CIS software and put it on the market as a Customer Information Control System, or CICS. Again the response was highly enthusiastic. Banks, insurance companies, and many other sorts of business had customer-service needs much like those of the Chicago utility.

All of IBM's IMS and CICS customers employed the systems in a hybrid batch/on-line system like the one in use at Rockwell. For example, a bank teller might engage the system in its on-line mode to answer a customer's question about the current balance in the customer's checking account. The teller might also record a deposit made by the customer. However, updating the account (adding the deposit, thus changing the balance) could wait until night, when the bank's computer updated all of the accounts in a single batch-processing job.

In the swiftly changing world of computer technology, CICS and IMS would prove remarkably durable. IBM modified them considerably over the years to meet the requirements of a broadening range of customers equipped with a wide variety of hardware, and by the mid-1980s, more than 25,000 data-processing installations around the world were using CICS or IMS-derived systems.

GETTING HELP IN A HURRY

Meanwhile, IBM's success with ACP among the airlines suggested its potential in opening up new markets for high-powered OLTP systems. One early—and at first glance unlikely—customer was the New York City Police Department. For decades, New York police had relied on an emergency-call system that had scarcely changed since the 1930s: A police operator responding to a citizen's request for help took the call, jotted down the information on a form, and passed it via conveyor belt to a radio dispatcher. This antiquated system was consigned to the junkyard with the coming of the computerized communications system called SPRINT. Installed in 1968 despite the barely concealed skepticism of veteran police officers—who collectively gave a silent cheer when the IBM 1401 computer failed to operate during its inaugural ceremonies—SPRINT soon won over its detractors by greatly increasing police efficiency.

New York officials had decided to invest in an ACP system because of the parallels between the on-line requirements of an airline and a big-city police department. One was the need for rapidity in handling transactions. Because ACP was designed from the ground up to include only the software required to handle its job, it was blindingly fast even in early versions. As one IBM official boasted, it ran like "a stripped-down stock car streamlined for speed." By the 1980s, an advanced version of ACP would run an expanded SABRE network of 80,000 terminals worldwide and could juggle 1,500 transactions per second during peak reservation times.

But the parallels went beyond speed. Citizens calling 911 are like passengers seeking seats on an airline flight. The operator was like the reservation clerk. Instead of flight numbers and seats, the single large data base would store information about the city—its streets and landmarks and the location of police resources at any given instant.

SPRINT operations revolve around five control rooms, each corresponding to one of the city's five boroughs. In each control room, sixty emergency operators and 100 radio dispatchers work quietly but intensely before a battery of computer terminals. Every incoming call is initially screened by a component of the telephone system called an ACD, or Automatic Call Distributor, which identifies the call's borough of origin and passes it to the appropriate control room, polling each operator in turn until it finds one with an open line.

On receiving a call, an operator first determines its exact location and the nature of the problem. The operator then logs the call, categorizes it according to a standard police code ("10/30" for "robbery in progress," for instance), and takes down other essential information such as an assailant's description, weapons, and direction of flight. All this appears in a standardized format on the terminal screen.

The computer assists in the recording and analysis of information by identifying and correcting human errors. Its memory, for example, contains special files that cross-reference the old and new names of places. A longtime resident of Queens may refer to 101st Avenue by its former name of Jerome Avenue, but if the operator types "Jerome Avenue" into the computer, the screen automatically displays it as 101st Avenue. The computer can also correct common misspellings of place or street names, again avoiding potential confusion. Still another file in the system's memory lists thirteen categories of places such as schools, hotels, theaters, and parks, and, when queried, it can display their exact locations.

Once any errors have been corrected and the call has been accepted by SPRINT, the computer assigns it an action priority (a holdup takes precedent over a cat stuck in a tree, for instance), determines the nearest available patrol car plus alternate units, and flashes the information to the dispatcher responsible for the sector where the call originated. The dispatcher's terminal displays the information on a split screen—the top half containing essential "what-and-where" information and the bottom half listing the local police units on hand. One or more units are alerted by radio and directed to the scene. Based on its knowledge of the responding unit's proximity to the emergency, SPRINT calculates how long it should take for the police to arrive. An internal clock keeps track of the time and prompts the dispatcher if the unit becomes overdue.

Another nonairline customer to recognize the advantage of ACP was BankAmericard, one of the first major distributors of credit cards (its name was changed to VISA in 1977). The postwar generation of Americans was the most mobile in history, and this roving society thrived on the easy credit symbolized by the ubiquitous plastic cards. Credit card checks, however, became increasingly difficult to perform as their use expanded.

Running a credit authorization was not a problem as long as a card was used within the territory of the issuing bank; handed a credit card by a customer, a store clerk had only to telephone the bank to make sure the card was valid and the holder's account good. But if the customer was from out of town—say a visitor from North Dakota making a purchase in Los Angeles—an authorization check was much more complicated. Prior to on-line transaction processing, long-distance authorization depended on telex messages shuttled back and forth between one regional authorization center and another. The process took at least five minutes to complete and could only be done at certain times of day.

To improve out-of-territory checking capabilities for its credit cards, BankAmericard in 1973 installed a customized transaction-processing system. Designed by IBM and using a System 370 model 138 computer, the system was designated BASE 1. Merchants requesting a credit check on BASE 1 were connected by telephone lines to local banks, which forwarded the request electronically to computers called MIPs (for Member Interface Processors) at regional authorization centers and ultimately to BankAmericard's central data base, located in San Mateo, California. The round-trip transaction took just a little more than a minute, and the service was available twenty-four hours a day, seven days a week.

Over the next several years, the number of bank credit cards issued and the capacity for swift credit checks grew hand in hand. BankAmericard's original BASE 1 could handle 5,000 transactions per hour during peak business hours. When the company installed new hardware and an improved operating system in 1977, volume jumped immediately to 13,000 transactions per hour. By 1978, the system was handling 200,000 transactions a day, most of them requiring two seconds or less of CPU time to complete. Moreover, the cost of processing each authorization had shrunk to one-fourth of the 1973 figure—from thirty cents per transaction to less than eight cents.

THE ON-LINE BOOM

By the mid-1970s, on-line transaction processing had become indispensible to several industries and was rapidly penetrating many others. This expansion was due largely to the development of more sophisticated software that had the ability to handle the increasingly complex and varied functions required of OLTP systems. Programmers had become more experienced and could build on the knowledge gained from first- and second-generation systems such as SABRE, PARS and CICS.

Another key factor was the advent of minicomputers—small, fast machines that were relatively inexpensive compared to the previous generation of mainframes. As costs plunged, both businesses and public institutions found that they could afford a host of OLTP applications for managing their data. In 1973, for example, OLTP invaded the neighborhood grocery store. That year the supermarket industry adopted the Universal Product Code (UPC)—printed patterns of bars that identified each item and that could be read and decoded by laser scanners installed in check-out counters. The identifying information was automatically sent to the store's computer, where the price of every article available in the store was kept up-to-date; almost instantly, the price was dispatched to the check-out terminal for totaling.

Computerizing the check-out line was obviously a boon to impatient shoppers, but it was even more of a help to store managers. The OLTP system kept a running tally of every item in the store, providing precise sales statistics. It identified fast-selling articles that deserved extra shelf space and lagging products that could be eliminated. More importantly, the instantaneous and constant inventory check allowed automatic ordering, so that the store was far less likely to run out of any particular item.

From grocery markets, the system spread to other retail outlets and to such major computer users as the U.S. Defense Department, the automobile industry, and hospitals—all of which depend on fast, accurate inventory control. By the late 1970s, telephone companies had begun to use OLTP systems to keep their directories current and to make the information in them more accessible to the public. When a customer called the familiar 411 number seeking directory assistance, the operator—instead of leafing by hand through a phone book—typed in the request to a data base containing all the phone numbers in a given area. A computer linked to a voice synthesizer then completed the transaction by reading the number requested. Another traditional institution, the public library, opened its doors to OLTP at this same time, and people seeking books found that on-line transaction terminals had begun to replace the old-fashioned card catalogs.

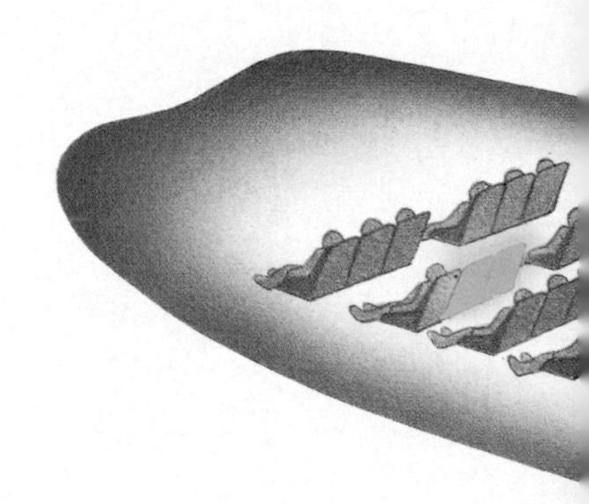

A RESERVATION ENGINE

Yet it was the original users that remained the most affected by the new technology. The airlines had come to depend on it absolutely, and their service had been transformed as a result of it. As OLTP reservation systems grew, designers continued to add new features to them. Clerks at SABRE terminals, for example, could book flights not only on their own airline but on other carriers as well. A reservation clerk could reserve a hotel room, a seat on a train, or a berth on an ocean liner; rent an automobile; purchase theater tickets and travel insurance; credit a frequent-flier account; or send a telex message anywhere in the world.

SABRE grew physically as well. From a single computer the system expanded to four powerful IBM 9083s sharing the load and providing backup against system failure. Its electronic network reached across the United States and to several distant countries on 550,000 miles of wire—enough to reach as far as the moon and back.

By 1979, IBM had decided to change the name of its generic Airline Control Program to emphasize its potential for nonairline uses. So ACP became TPF, for Transaction Processing Facility. And indeed, other industries saddled with complicated reservation systems were natural customers for TPF.

Hotel chains were among the first to see the opportunity. In 1980 the Holiday Corporation, parent company of Holiday Inns, Hampton Inns, and Embassy Suites, installed a TPF system called Holidex to serve its international network of 210 hotels and 44,000 rooms. Holidex could process 70,000 messages per second on an IBM 3083 mainframe. Like other OLTP systems, Holidex shuttled between one user and the next according to a prioritized sequence, giving each user the illusion of having exclusive access to the computer. It moved records between a permanent off-line memory (stored on disks) and a main on-line memory. And it controlled access to the data base by matching user queries from a specific terminal with the type of information that would normally be requested from that terminal.

An agent typing a request to rent a room initiated a complex sequence of events on Holidex. Suppose a customer at the Holiday Inn in Washington, D.C., asked to reserve a room with a king-size bed at the Chicago North Holiday Inn

two weeks hence, on April 5. When the agent queried the data base about the availability of such a room, the system went to main memory, where it looked at a terminal control record to be sure the user was legitimate, and to format the screen appropriately for the information requested. Then TPF located a record of room inventory for all hotels in the system and extracted from it the Chicago North room inventory for the week of April 5. It next checked the availability of a room with a king-size bed on that date, and if a room was available, TPF would automatically make the reservation and reduce the room inventory by one. The entire process took just two seconds of computer time—far less than the time it takes to read this explanation of how it was done.

Such advances in computerized reservations systems have enabled the commercial aviation industry to keep up with the ongoing boom in air travel. Today, the world's airlines carry more than 400 million passengers a year, and four-fifths of those travelers buy their tickets from travel agents using OLTPs. American Airlines, which had been first to get into the field, continues to dominate it. American began marketing its SABRE service to travel agents in 1976, and, from its underground, disaster-proof computer center in Tulsa, Oklahoma, American still processes nearly half of the computer-booked airline reservations made each day.

Except for the U.S. Government, American Airlines has the largest on-line transaction-processing computer system in the world. The overall market for OLTP has continued to grow without pause. During the first half of the 1980s, sales of OLTP systems jumped fourfold to well over a hundred thousand units a year. In this same period, the average price per unit diminished almost 50 percent. Despite this reduction in price—or possibly because of it—the worldwide annual market for OLTP systems now stands at about $25 billion, and it is expected to double within a few years. A single startling fact tells the tale: sales of the hardware and software for on-line transaction processing has already outstripped the entire semiconductor industry.

Data Bases: Facts on File

2

Computer-managed data bases are the workhorses of the information age. These extensively cross-referenced record-keeping systems have become indispensable tools in a wide variety of applications. Their uses range from such glamorous assignments as helping police track down fugitive criminals to the more mundane chores of assembling mailing lists, monitoring inventories, and preparing employee payrolls.

The first data bases, developed during the 1950s, were simple file systems, the computerized counterparts of document-crammed folders in a drawer; files were limited in size, and there was little flexibility in the way the data could be organized or what applications could be served. But increases in computer storage capacity spawned ever more sophisticated approaches to managing a steadily growing mass of facts and figures. Today's data-base systems provide access to enormous volumes of information, readily accommodating all sorts of requests.

Three basic models for organizing electronic records have guided data-base development. Hierarchical data bases exhibit a branching structure, with information arranged into sets and subsets; getting to a particular piece of data may require going through several vertically ordered files, a process akin to finding a distant cousin on a family tree. Network data bases offer many more direct connections between files, but—as in hierarchies—the links are preordained and are difficult to change or adjust.

Relational data bases, in contrast, not only accommodate multiple connections but allow new links to be forged as needs arise—by far the most flexible approach to data management. The following pages illustrate how a relational data base would serve a small university, typical of many organizations in the diversity of its information needs.

A Data-Base System for the University

A university—like a bank, an insurance company, or a department of the government—is a complex organization, administered by numerous offices that all have their own informational needs.

As exemplified by the fictional odyssey below, a university's administrative structure can seem bafflingly convoluted (a veritable nightmare to a new student) if paperwork is the

In a university that lacks a data base to manage information, a new student begins a seemingly endless paper chase when she picks up registration forms at the admissions building and goes to the office of her faculty adviser, who approves her course choices. But at the registrar's office, she learns that the payments she has made do not cover tuition, and she is sent to arrange a payment plan with the finance office, where she finds out that she is eligible for a job. But campus employment is arranged by the personnel office. There, the student is assigned a job and given a form to present at the finance office certifying her ability to pay. She returns to the registrar with the forms she has amassed—and completes yet another form to enroll in classes.

Compiling data dictionaries

To create a computerized record-keeping system tailored to the university's needs, a data-base administrator asks each office to list the information it requires and how it uses these facts. These lists, or data dictionaries, ensure that all departments' information needs are addressed during development of the data base.

Refining the entries

Deluged with detail, the data-base administrator reviews the data dictionaries, eliminating redundant entries, giving each item a standard name and precise definition, and arranging items in useful categories. The result is a single data dictionary that serves as a reference for the entire university.

Diagramming a structure

Having agreed with the university on a relational data base, the administrator diagrams its structure, detailing the interconnections between categories. The result is akin to a map that shows how one university office can acquire information maintained by another.

only link between the parts. But there is a powerful electronic alternative: a relational data base. The creation of such a unified information system is described by the sequence of steps at the bottom of these pages. (Typically, the task of building the system would be entrusted to a specialist called a data-base administrator.) How the system works is explained on the pages that follow.

The benefits of a relational data base to a university—or any equivalent organization—are immense. The system allows the university's many offices to gather large amounts of information with little duplication and small risk of error. And because each office has instant access to facts compiled by the others, complex matters involving many parties can be worked out in a trice at a single terminal.

Programming the design
Next, the administrator uses a data-base programming language to specify the name for each item to be included in the data base and whether the item is to be text (the title of a course, for example) or a number to be used mathematically (payments or hours worked, for instance).

Loading the system
Finally, information is loaded into the data base by typing it at terminals or copying it from tape. The administrator then oversees the system's operation, ensuring, among other things, that space on disk drives is adequate and that data is copied onto tape to guard against computer malfunction.

Data by the Tableful

A relational data base stores facts in tables called relations *(below)*. The only requirement of the information is that it must be capable of being laid out in rows and columns (like a pencil-and-paper roster of names, addresses, and telephone numbers). Since virtually every kind of data can meet this criterion, relational data bases can be adapted to almost any record-keeping purpose.

The relations displayed on the opposite page represent a much simplified university data base. Each facet of the university's administration is symbolized by a table that contains information within the purview of a single department. The admissions office, for example, keeps track of students by ID number, name, and major field of study. The personnel department records the department, rank, names, and social security numbers of the teaching staff, and so on.

Isolated from one another, these tables would be nothing more than a simple, computerized filing system. Tied together, however, they become a data base, each table offering access to the information held by all the others. This versatility stems from deliberate duplication of columns in two or more tables, resulting in a tool called a common key. If, for example, two tables containing information about students each possess a column containing student ID numbers—no two of which are alike—then an ID number can be used to find the row in each table that contains information applicable to any student.

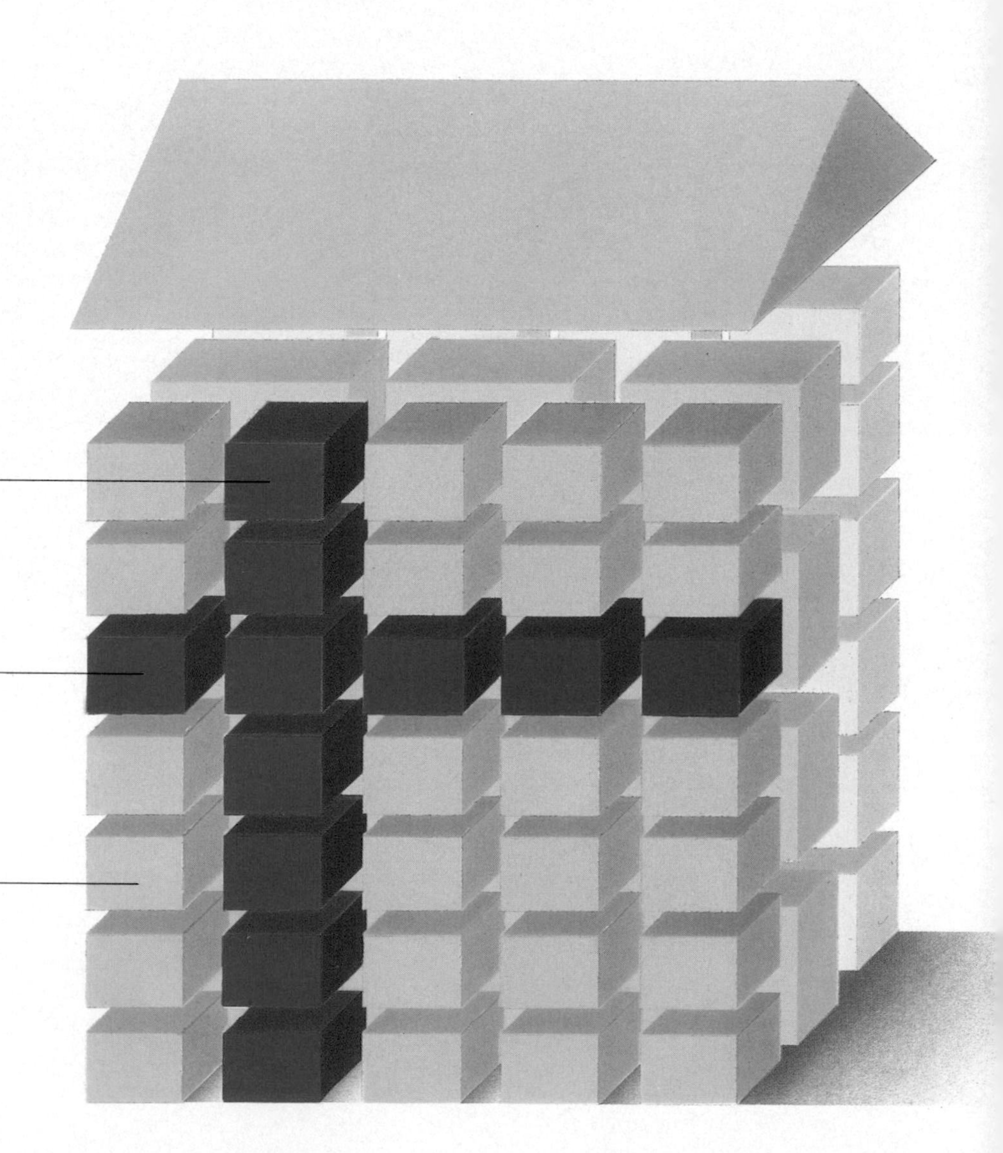

An attribute
Each column in a table represents a single attribute, or characteristic, of the table's subject. A column might contain, for example, the identity numbers of the students or each professor's department.

A record
Each row, or record, in a table contains all the information about a single entry. In the case of a student, a record might include, in addition to an identity number, the individual's first and last names and major course of study.

An occurrence
Belonging to both a row and a column, an occurrence is the basic unit of a relational data-base table. It contains the value of an attribute for a single record; in some cases, the value is a string of letters making up a word or words, in others a set of numerals—such as a student's ID number.

2

Admissions Office

STUDENTS

StudentId	LastName	FirstName	Dept
7016639	Morgan	George	Engl
0010534	Deal	Sue	Math
9105977	Conrad	Mark	Hist
2053021	McDowell	Tina	Chem
4344891	Gomez	David	Bio
0355703	Frear	Robert	Engl
9470825	Whitney	Pam	Fr
3171386	Smith	Steven	Bio
8200461	Heinz	Judith	Engl

Personnel Office

STAFF

Dept	Rank	LastName	FirstName	Ssn
Engl	Asso	Register	Chris	009114622
Bio	Asst	Cohn	Denise	417825508
Math	Prof	York	Carla	660481233
Chem	Asst	Sawyer	John	444203951
Fr	Inst	Durham	Paul	010669325
Engl	Prof	Syng	Kim	003661690
Chem	Prof	Franco	Henry	455020016
Hist	Inst	Preston	Lydia	911522670
Bio	Asso	Kelly	Susan	620031192

Finance Office

CLASSROOMS

Bldg	Room	Dept	Section
Thompson	210	Hist	2943
Seeley	34	Engl	2107
Douglas	308	Chem	3376
Wright	15	Fr	5601
Douglas	112	Bio	3641
Douglas	225	Math	4603
Thompson	120	Engl	5864
Wright	31	Bio	3780
Thompson	233	Engl	1885

Registrar's Office

REGISTRATION

Section	StudentId
5601	9105977
3376	2053021
2107	7016639
4603	3171386
3780	4344891
1885	8200461
3641	0010534
1885	9470825
2943	8200461

Faculty Office

COURSES

Dept	Course	Credit	Section
Engl	101	3	2107
Fr	210	3	5601
Math	300	3	4603
Chem	305	4	3376
Bio	110	4	3641
Engl	280	3	5864
Hist	212	3	2943
Engl	101	3	1885
Bio	110	4	3780

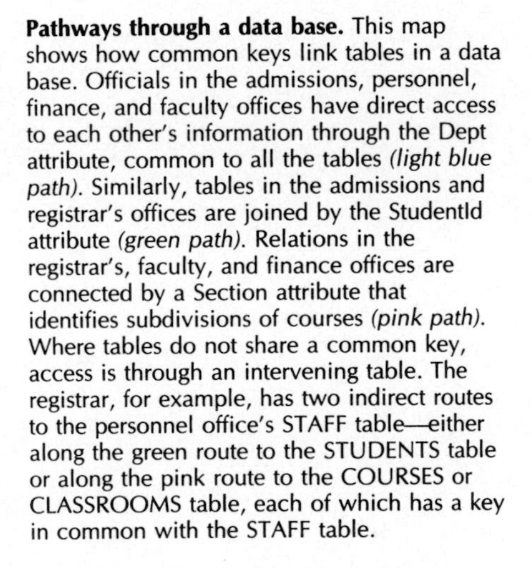

Pathways through a data base. This map shows how common keys link tables in a data base. Officials in the admissions, personnel, finance, and faculty offices have direct access to each other's information through the Dept attribute, common to all the tables *(light blue path)*. Similarly, tables in the admissions and registrar's offices are joined by the StudentId attribute *(green path)*. Relations in the registrar's, faculty, and finance offices are connected by a Section attribute that identifies subdivisions of courses *(pink path)*. Where tables do not share a common key, access is through an intervening table. The registrar, for example, has two indirect routes to the personnel office's STAFF table—either along the green route to the STUDENTS table or along the pink route to the COURSES or CLASSROOMS table, each of which has a key in common with the STAFF table.

The Answer Depends upon the Question

Success in extracting information from a data base rests on posing just the right question, a precisely worded query that specifies the steps that the data-base management system must perform to assemble the information. In general, the more restrictive the request—that is, the less information sought—or the more tables that a request sends the computer searching through, the lengthier the query. For example, a request for all the information in all the records of a single table may require a query of only a few words. In contrast, asking for selected attributes for a few records chosen from multiple tables may tax the skill of the most accomplished data-base manipulator.

Whether simple or complex, a data-base query must be perfectly phrased. A comma misplaced, a space added, or a word misspelled while typing the question at the computer terminal may produce no results at all or, even worse, may yield an answer that is incomplete or otherwise incorrect in some undetectable way.

Questions are addressed to data bases in a variety of languages. The examples on these and the following pages explain how a computer processes requests written in SQL (Structured Query Language), a popular language developed by IBM data-base specialists. Key words, such as SELECT, FROM, and WHERE, tell the computer what operations to perform on the tables, attributes, and individual values named in the query. Although SQL's full lexicon covers a wide range of functions—from counting and averaging to updating and expanding—the examples here concentrate on a few critical operations: calling up and merging tables, setting conditions to target specific records, and selecting which attributes the answer should include.

The computer's response is itself a table, which is displayed on the user's screen and may be named and stored in the data base for easy recall. More complicated requests, such as the one on pages 60-61, typically combine several simpler statements, so the computer actually creates a sequence of temporary tables as it works through the phrases, making preliminary selections of records and attributes before going on to home in on the final result.

While mastering a query language ensures the greatest flexibility in using a data base, some systems offer less daunting approaches. Common requests can be preprogrammed into the system and made available through simple commands. Or the user may be prompted by the computer with a series of options that eventually pin down the information being sought. Such menu-driven systems give even the infrequent information seeker relatively unfettered access to the resources of a data base.

SQL: SELECT ALL FROM STAFF WHERE RANK = "PROF"

Personnel Office

STAFF

Dept	Rank	LastName	FirstName	Ssn
Engl	Asso	Register	Chris	009114622
Bio	Asst	Cohn	Denise	417825508
Math	Prof	York	Carla	660481233
Chem	Asst	Sawyer	John	444203951
Fr	Inst	Durham	Paul	010669325
Engl	Prof	Syng	Kim	003661690
Chem	Prof	Franco	Henry	455020016
Hist	Inst	Preston	Lydia	911522670
Bio	Asso	Kelly	Susan	620031192

Dept	Rank	Last Name	First Name	Ssn
Math	Prof	York	Carla	660481233
Engl	Prof	Syng	Kim	003661690
Chem	Prof	Franco	Henry	455020016

A single, simple condition. For a review of university staffing patterns, a personnel officer asks the computer to identify all professors. The SQL version of this query, shown above, consists of three distinct phrases, each representing a separate operation. Cued by the word FROM, the computer first locates a table named STAFF, then goes about satisfying the condition expressed in the phrase WHERE RANK = "PROF": It examines each record, retaining in its temporary memory only those with a value of "Prof" in the Rank column. The query's opening phrase, SELECT ALL, instructs the computer to list the full set of five attributes in the three-record table that appears on the screen of the personnel officer's terminal.

SQL: SELECT LASTNAME, FIRSTNAME, FROM STUDENTS WHERE DEPT = "ENGL"

Admissions Office

STUDENTS

StudentId	LastName	FirstName	Dept
7016639	Morgan	George	Engl
0010534	Deal	Sue	Math
9105977	Conrad	Mark	Hist
2053021	McDowell	Tina	Chem
4344891	Gomez	David	Bio
0355703	Frear	Robert	Engl
9470825	Whitney	Pam	Fr
3171386	Smith	Steven	Bio
8200461	Heinz	Judith	Engl

Last Name	First Name
Morgan	George
Frear	Robert
Heinz	Judith

Specifying attributes. To obtain a list of the names of students majoring in English, the chairman of the department poses the above query to the data base. After locating the admissions office's STUDENTS table, the computer identifies the three records that meet the condition of containing the value "Engl" in the Dept column. The query also directs the computer to select only two of the four attributes in the table, those listing students' last and first names; the two other unspecified attributes are disregarded. Thus, the final answer displayed at the chairman's terminal includes no extraneous information.

SQL: SELECT ALL FROM CLASSROOMS WHERE DEPT = "ENGL" AND BLDG = "THOMPSON"

Finance Office

CLASSROOMS

Bldg	Room	Dept	Section
Thompson	210	Hist	2943
Seeley	34	Engl	2107
Douglas	308	Chem	3376
Wright	15	Fr	5601
Douglas	112	Bio	3641
Douglas	225	Math	4603
Thompson	120	Engl	5864
Wright	31	Bio	3780
Thompson	233	Engl	1885

Bldg	Room	Dept	Section
Thompson	120	Engl	5864
Thompson	233	Engl	1885

Satisfying dual conditions. The English department chairman also wants to know what rooms in Thompson Hall are assigned to the department. The university's data dictionary, which lists all of the data base's tables and their attributes, indicates that a table named CLASSROOMS—maintained by the finance office—holds the necessary information. The query therefore instructs the computer to call up that table, then specifies a pair of conditions for choosing records: DEPT = "ENGL" AND BLDG = "THOMPSON." Reading through the whole table, the computer extracts only those records that satisfy both requirements; it displays all of the attributes for the two applicable records because of the query's stipulation to SELECT ALL.

```
SQL: SELECT LASTNAME, FIRSTNAME, FROM STUDENTS WHERE STUDENTID IN SELECT
STUDENTID FROM REGISTRATION, COURSES
WHERE DEPT="ENGL" AND COURSE="101" AND REGISTRATION.SECTION = COURSES.SECTION
```

Registrar's Office

REGISTRATION

Section	StudentId
5601	9105977
3376	2053021
2107	7016639
4603	3171386
3780	4344891
1885	8200461
3641	0010534
1885	9470825
2943	8200461

Faculty Office

COURSES

Dept	Course	Credit	Section
Engl	101	3	2107
Fr	210	3	5601
Math	300	3	4603
Chem	305	4	3376
Bio	110	4	3641
Engl	280	3	5864
Hist	212	3	2943
Engl	101	3	1885
Bio	110	4	3780

1 The lengthy query above asks a simple question: Who is taking English 101? Because no single table contains all the data required, a necessary first step is to join the REGISTRATION and COURSES tables *(above),* which share the attribute Section as a common key. The query's last phrase sets the condition: Combine those records from the two named tables whose Section values match; the sixth record in COURSES is thus excluded because no students are registered for section 5864.

Section	StudentId	Dept	Course	Credit
5601	9105977	Fr	210	3
3376	2053021	Chem	305	4
2107	7016639	Engl	101	3
4603	3171386	Math	300	3
3780	4344891	Bio	110	4
1885	8200461	Engl	101	3
3641	0010534	Bio	110	4
1885	9470825	Engl	101	3
2943	8200461	Hist	212	3

2 The resulting combined table, held in the computer's temporary memory, includes three important attributes that will be used to process the query further: StudentId, Dept, and Course. The computer can now advance to the pair of conditions expressed in the phrase WHERE DEPT = "ENGL" AND COURSE = "101," ferreting out the three records that fulfill both requirements.

Section	StudentId	Dept	Course	Credit
2107	7016639	Engl	101	3
1885	8200461	Engl	101	3
1885	9470825	Engl	101	3

Section	StudentId	Dept	Course	Credit
2107	7016639	Engl	101	3
1885	8200461	Engl	101	3
1885	9470825	Engl	101	3

3 The three records selected in the last search are assembled in a second temporary table, as shown at top. Instructed to SELECT STUDENTID, the computer focuses on that attribute alone *(above, bottom);* it will serve as the common key linking the temporary table with the admissions office's STUDENTS table *(right),* which contains the names ultimately sought in the query.

2

Admissions Office

STUDENTS

StudentId	LastName	FirstName	Dept
7016639	Morgan	George	Engl
0010534	Deal	Sue	Math
9105977	Conrad	Mark	Hist
2053021	McDowell	Tina	Chem
4344891	Gomez	David	Bio
0355703	Frear	Robert	Engl
9470825	Whitney	Pam	Fr
3171386	Smith	Steven	Bio
8200461	Heinz	Judith	Engl

4 The computer next turns to the phrase FROM STUDENTS, locating the STUDENTS table in storage. It then satisfies the condition WHERE STUDENTID IN by finding the three records whose student identification numbers match those from the temporary table at left.

StudentId	LastName	FirstName	Dept
7016639	Morgan	George	Engl
8200461	Heinz	Judith	Engl
9470825	Whitney	Pam	Fr

StudentId	LastName	FirstName	Dept
7016639	Morgan	George	Engl
8200461	Heinz	Judith	Engl
9470825	Whitney	Pam	Fr

5 The specified records form a table with four columns *(top),* but only two—LastName and FirstName—pertain to the user's request. The computer selects those attributes *(bottom),* discards the other two, and displays a final table *(right)* containing just what was asked for: the names of the students enrolled in English 101.

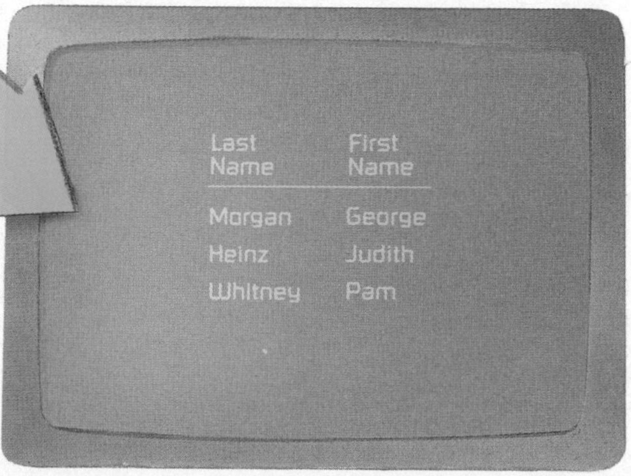

Last Name	First Name
Morgan	George
Heinz	Judith
Whitney	Pam

Shortcuts to the Data

Both for a person seeking information from a data base and for the computer that must find it, time is a precious commodity. Sequential searches, such as those explained on the previous pages, involve a laborious ritual: The computer reviews tables from top to bottom, retrieving one record after another to identify those that contain the desired information. Given that tables may run a million or more records long, this can be an extremely inefficient and time-consuming method of retrieving data.

Fortunately, data-base administrators can expedite searches with several strategies, two of which are illustrated on

SQL: SELECT ALL FROM COURSES WHERE SECTION = "3780"

Faculty Office

COURSES

Dept	Course	Credit	Section
Engl	101	3	1885
Engl	101	3	2107
Hist	212	3	2943
Chem	305	4	3376
Bio	110	4	3641
Bio	110	4	3780
Math	300	3	4603
Fr	210	3	5601
Engl	280	3	5864

Faculty Office

COURSES

Dept	Course	Credit	Section
Engl	101	3	1885
Engl	101	3	2107
Hist	212	3	2943
Chem	305	4	3376
Bio	110	4	3641
Bio	110	4	3780
Math	300	3	4603
Fr	210	3	5601
Engl	280	3	5864

Faculty Office

COURSES

Dept	Course	Credit	Section
Engl	101	3	1885
Engl	101	3	2107
Hist	212	3	2943
Chem	305	4	3376
Bio	110	4	3641
Bio	110	4	3780
Math	300	3	4603
Fr	210	3	5601
Engl	280	3	5864

A binary search. Instructed to retrieve information about section 3780, the computer uses the fact that the Section values are numerically ordered to find its quarry. Rather than starting at the top of the COURSES table, it goes to the middle *(above, left)* and makes a comparison, determining that the data value 3641 is less than the one it is seeking. Because of the numerical ordering, the computer knows that all the records above the middle one are also too low. It goes to the middle of the remaining half—here, the second of the bottom four records *(above, center)*; it finds that 4603 is too high and removes the records below from consideration. The winnowing process leaves only one option *(above, right)*, and the correct record is promptly displayed on the questioner's screen *(right)*.

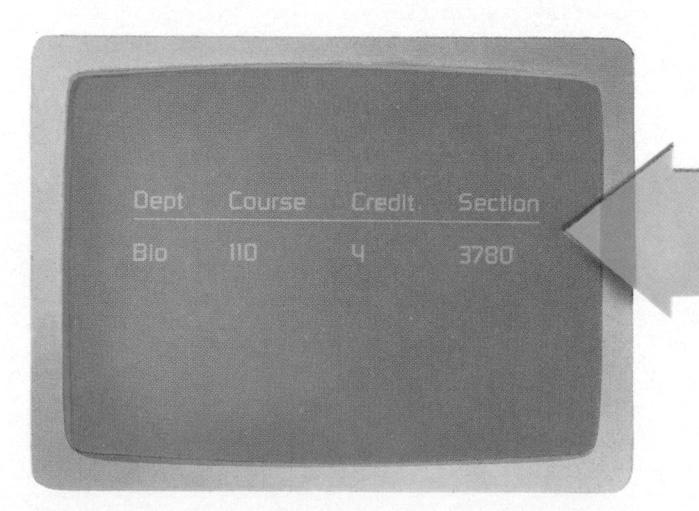

these pages. For binary searching, the administrator must ensure that the data values for a selected attribute are in either numerical or alphabetical order. The computer then homes in on data by dividing the table into successively smaller halves; after each division, the computer determines whether the targeted value lies above or below the dividing line and eliminates the other half from further searching, a process that can quickly narrow the range of possible choices down to one.

Indexing *(below)* saves even more time. For certain attributes, the DBA creates an index—in this case, a two-column table that lists in one column the specific data values for that attribute and in the other the coded addresses of all the records where each value may be found. Whenever a specific value is named in a query, the computer simply looks up its address in the index and then goes straight to the appropriate record or records, without wasting time reading through all of them. Of course, the computer has to search through the index table itself, so a binary search or other time-saving method must also be used. But because indexes are generally smaller than full tables, the computer still gets where it needs to go much faster.

SQL: SELECT ALL FROM COURSES WHERE SECTION = "3780"

INDEX ON SECTION

Section	Reference
1885	5 R8, 3 R9, 4 R6, R8
2107	5 R1, 3 R2, 4 R3
2943	5 R7, 3 R1, 4 R9
3376	5 R4, 3 R3, 4 R2
3641	5 R5, 3 R5, 4 R7
3780	5 R9, 3 R8 4 R5
4603	5 R3, 3 R6 4 R4
5601	5 R2, 3 R4, 4 R1
5864	5 R6, 3 R7

Faculty Office

COURSES

Dept	Course	Credit	Section
Engl	101	3	2107
Fr	210	3	5601
Math	300	3	4603
Chem	305	4	3376
Bio	110	4	3641
Engl	280	3	5864
Hist	212	3	2943
Engl	101	3	1885
Bio	110	4	3780

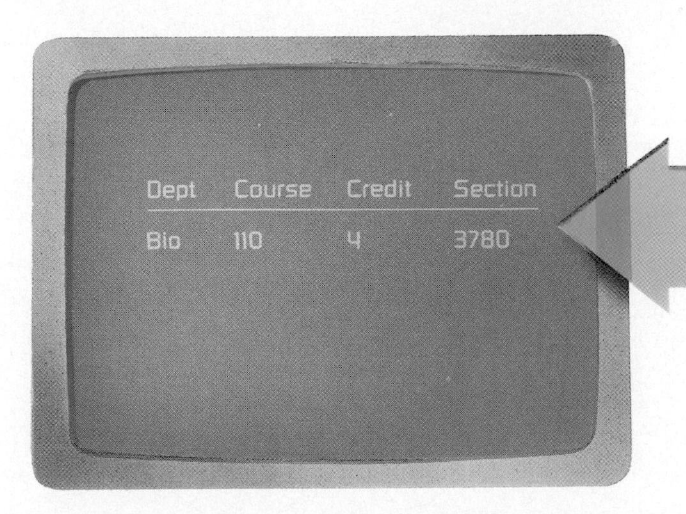

Using an index. To speed the answering of the same query, the computer first consults the table INDEX ON SECTION *(above)* and locates the record that contains section 3780. Once there, it reads the coded addresses in the Reference column, looks for the number 5—the code number for the COURSES table named in the query—and finds the reference R9. The ninth record in the COURSES table is retrieved in one trip to the data base *(right),* instead of the nine it would take for a sequential search.

Failure-Proofing the Computer

3

The proliferation of OLTP terminals at tellers' windows and ticket counters that began in 1964 with the introduction of American Airlines' SABRE reservation system created a new problem for businessmen: When their on-line computers stopped, their businesses stopped. As recently as the mid-1970s, most computer installations could be expected to halt unexpectedly at least once a year because of a hardware malfunction or because of problems with software; some computers failed every three or four months.

In a batch-processing operation, where data gathered from various sources over the course of a day or a week was processed all at once, an occasional instance of computer failure represented a relatively minor setback. Users did not expect immediate results and, unless there was already a backlog of work, lost time usually could be recovered by running the computers overtime. But in an on-line system, from which immediate response was expected, computer failure for even a few minutes resulted in angry customers and could spell immediate losses to a business. An airline with a computer down could book no additional passengers; a store with inoperative cash-register terminals could not sell its merchandise. Even worse, when a computer stopped in mid-transaction, valuable data such as the record of a deposit to a bank account might be lost or destroyed.

The only safeguard against a disastrous computer failure lay in redundant systems, in which one machine was backed up by another that stood by as understudy to the primary computer. Setting up such a system was an expensive undertaking that involved buying multiple computers and that, in most cases, required investing substantially in customized hardware and software to link the machines together. By 1975, businesses dependent on OLTP systems were spending an estimated $200 million dollars a year to build and maintain redundant systems—an expenditure that was expected to rise by some 35 percent annually.

In Santa Clara, California, however, a little-known start-up company named Tandem Computers had been working on a proposal for a less costly solution to the problem of computer failure: a unique all-in-one hardware-software package designed expressly for OLTP. The package would consist of a computer and an operating system with built-in mechanisms to ensure that the processing of transactions could continue despite the failure of any single hardware or software component.

At the outset, the company had little to show potential customers except for the professional biographies of its founders. But for savvy industry watchers, those résumés held great promise: Some of the fledgling firm's top engineers and key executives were émigrés from Hewlett-Packard, a highly regarded California electronics company that had entered the computer business less than a decade earlier and that was already on the way to becoming one of the world's leading suppliers of midsized machines for business and industry.

The president of the new company—and the man who had recruited the others—was a former marketing manager of Hewlett-Packard's minicomputer division, Jim Treybig, a 35-year-old East Texan who was better known to his associates as Jimmy T.

A BETTER IDEA

Treybig was not immediately recognizable as a successful businessman. His hair was an unruly frizz. Oversize glasses continually slipped down the bridge of his nose. Rebellious shirttails refused to stay neatly tucked around his stocky frame. But beneath the slightly rumpled appearance beat the heart of a gambler. A youthful passion for poker had left Treybig with a taste for risk and a healthy measure of self-confidence. Treybig had been schooled as an electrical engineer, acquiring a bachelor's degree in the subject from Rice University in 1964. Later, he earned a Master of Business Administration degree from Stanford. While studying there, he took up computer programming so that he could use the school's IBM mainframe to handicap the stock market. Thus by temperament and education, Treybig was well equipped to become a high-stakes entrepreneur of the computer age.

When Jimmy T. joined Hewlett-Packard in 1968, he found himself in one of the twentieth century's most fertile fields for someone of his qualities. The company's headquarters were located in Santa Clara County, where sleepy old orchards were rapidly disappearing beneath a carpet of high-tech laboratories and low-rise factories. The transformation was turning the region into what the world would soon come to know as Silicon Valley—the booming heart of the new microelectronics industry. An atmosphere of technological innovation and entrepreneurial fever pervaded the Valley. Inhaling it perhaps more deeply than most, Treybig saw a golden opportunity to snare some of the millions being spent on redundant computer systems.

Hewlett-Packard's customers, actual and potential, included banks and hotel chains and retail stores. On-line transaction systems would fill the bill for all of these business leaders, but they were wary of entrusting day-to-day operations to the fallible machines.

All computers are vulnerable to failure in a multitude of ways, any of which can disable an automated system. A speck of dust can cripple a disk drive, where irreplaceable data and programs may be stored. An electrical fault inside the computer can shut down the central processing unit. A bug hiding deep within an application program, or an unforeseen sequence of keystrokes can freeze the system in its tracks.

Redundant computer systems created to address these and other potentially serious issues were not only expensive—prohibitively so for small businesses—but they were and would remain a poor solution to the problem. Most fail-safe arrangements cobbled up for the commercial market were based on a principle called switched backup.

The simplest and least expensive form of switched backup holds in reserve a separate computer sometimes called a cold backup because it is not turned on unless the main computer fails. If that happens, a human operator starts the spare machine and then transfers the transaction processing load to it—a procedure that can take several hours. During that period of time, no transactions can be processed at all; throughout an OLTP system, the computer is down. Furthermore, with this arrangement it was difficult to reconstruct data lost when the computer stopped.

In a more advanced form of protection, the understudy computer (called a hot backup) runs in lockstep with the primary machine. If the primary machine fails, the operator must enter a series of commands to transfer the computing load to the reserve machine—a hand-off that can occur within minutes of a breakdown. But while a hot-backup system can result in less computer downtime than a cold-backup system, it is little better than the less expensive system at keeping track of data being processed at the instant of shutdown, and it is dauntingly complex to build.

Most computers and their operating systems are designed to run independently of other machines. This was particularly true in the 1960s and early 1970s, when virtually all of the computers operated by businesses were employed mainly in batch processing. Those machines made no provision for joining two of them together, an essential step in establishing a hot-backup system. More than a pair of wires, the connection of one CPU to another required the installation of specialized intercomputer communications equipment.

Hot-backup systems also entailed extensive modifications to the operating-system software. Most computers, then as now, could be programmed with relative ease to exchange data with one another. However, inducing one machine to pass an interrupted processing job smoothly to another demanded program-to-program communication between the two, that is, the facility for the operating system in one computer to accept messages from an operating system in another computer.

But operating systems are designed to give orders, not to receive them, so opening this communications channel required adding to both operating systems elaborate strings of commands telling one computer how and under what circumstances to accept messages from or send them to the other—a devilishly complex feat of software engineering.

Making such fundamental changes was not only a time-consuming and expensive enterprise—the cost of the software in a hot-backup system can easily exceed that of the hardware—but one that carried with it the risk of introducing a bug in the operating system, something as difficult to ferret out as an extra comma or a misplaced parenthesis, that could in itself cause a computer to fail. Furthermore, once such a system is up and running, it could not be easily updated or expanded, as computer installations often must be, in order to meet changing demands. Connecting additional peripheral devices or new software invariably called for further alterations to the operating system. Worst of all, even the simplest hardware or software change shut down the computer system while the upgraded components were installed.

Despite their importance to many industries, backup systems for OLTP operations formed only the smallest of niches in the computer market. In the early 1970s, as critical as on-line processing had become for many industries, the computer systems capable of this kind of work represented a relatively small share of the booming market for business computers. And the demand for more trustworthy on-line computer systems, although growing at an impressive rate, was smaller still. The major computer companies were committed to hardware

A Speedy System for Checking Credit

Convenience is the hallmark of a credit card, and computers have helped make the so-called plastic money easy to use anywhere in the world. Computerized authorization systems now approve or reject credit-card transactions within seconds, providing effective protection against fraud or abuse, with little effort on the part of the merchant and a minimum of delay to the customer.

Some automated schemes make do with simply checking a card's account number against a list of lost, stolen, or otherwise invalid cards; if a match is found, authorization of

An automated credit-card check begins and ends at an authorization terminal in the store *(below)*. The merchant first passes the credit card through a slot that reads the account number and expiration date coded on the magnetic stripe on the back; the keyboard is used to enter the purchase amount. Typically, the data is then automatically transmitted by phone lines to a computer at the merchant's bank, and from there through an international networking system to whichever bank holds the customer's credit account. After evaluating the request, the bank's computer returns its answer through the same channels. The terminal's display will show either a word such as "denied" or an approval code—here, the number 96440.

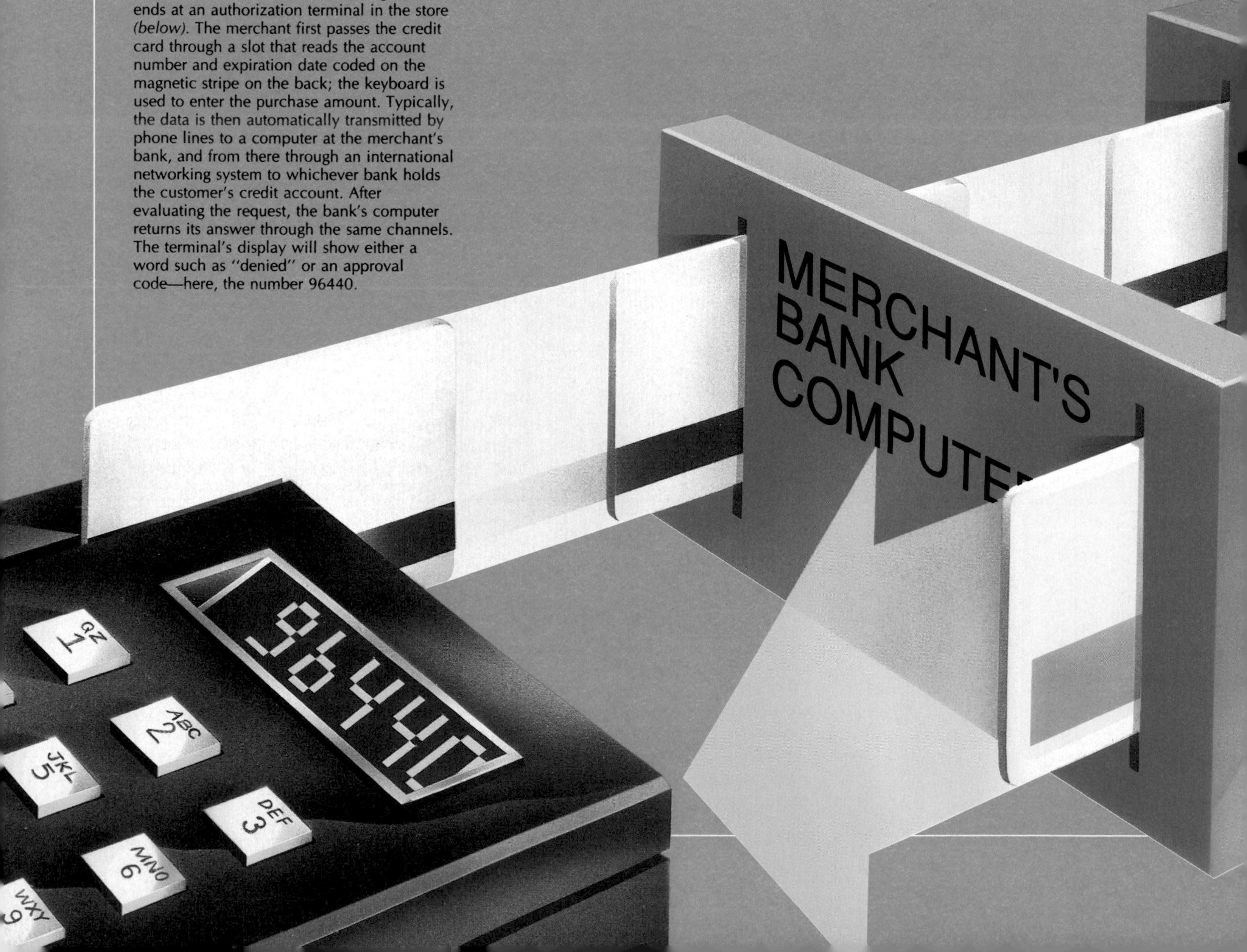

the transaction is denied. But a more comprehensive check—to determine, for example, whether a valid card has exceeded its credit limit—calls for examining the customer's actual credit file, typically stored in a data base maintained by the bank that issued the card. As the diagram below indicates, such an approach relies on the rapid exchange of electronic information between bank computers, accomplished through a communications network that links thousands of these data bases worldwide.

Individual storeowners hook into the network by way of their local bank's computer, reached through a specialized terminal *(below, left)* that automatically reads card numbers and dispatches authorization requests; the merchant need only punch a few keys to set the whole checking process in motion. In some cases, a credit-card service, which consolidates credit records from many different banks in one central data base, will handle the request. But even when a bank itself does the checking, an answer can appear on the terminal's display in less than ten seconds, a clear demonstration of the system's proficiency at both routing and processing data.

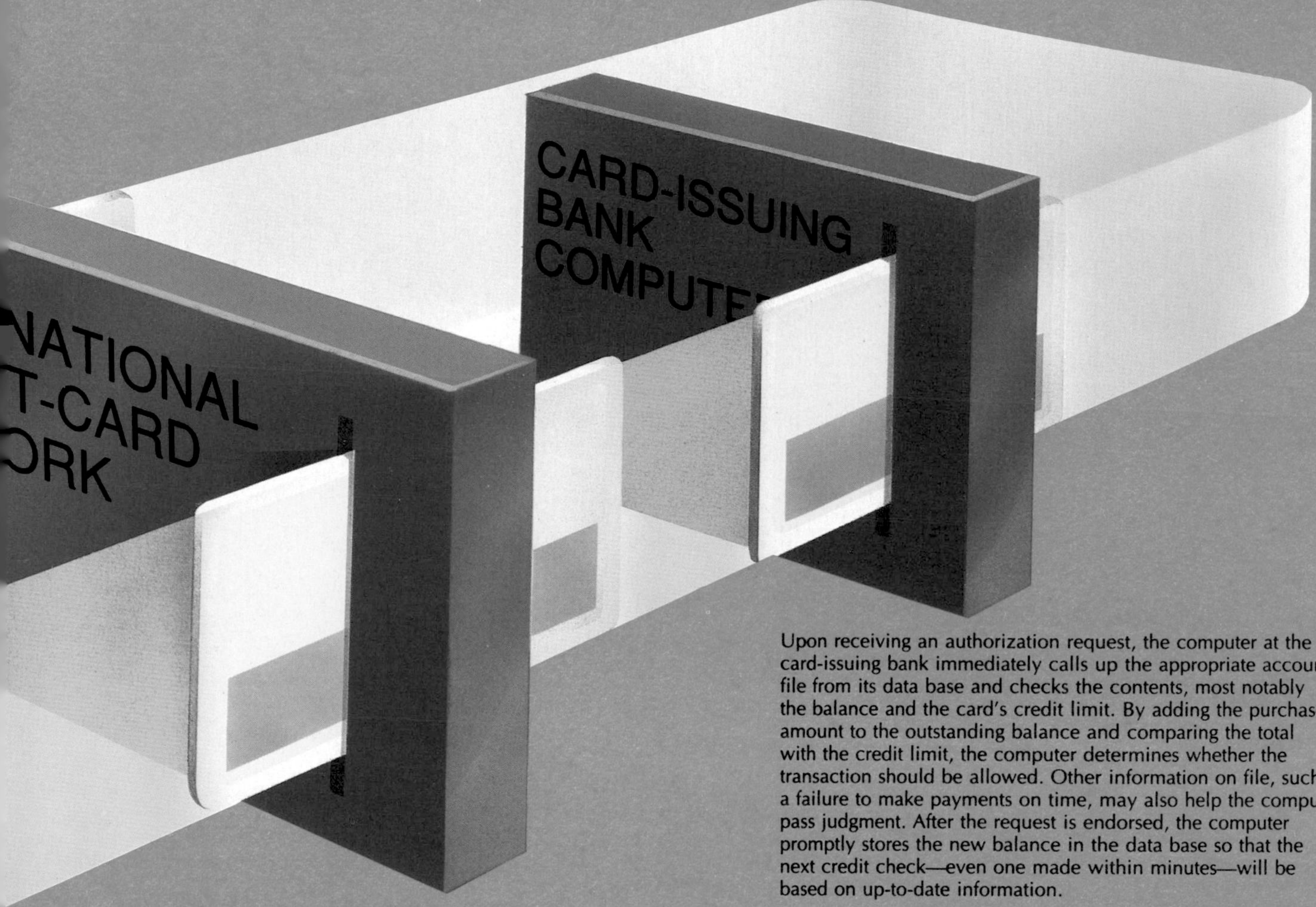

Upon receiving an authorization request, the computer at the card-issuing bank immediately calls up the appropriate account file from its data base and checks the contents, most notably the balance and the card's credit limit. By adding the purchase amount to the outstanding balance and comparing the total with the credit limit, the computer determines whether the transaction should be allowed. Other information on file, such as a failure to make payments on time, may also help the computer pass judgment. After the request is endorsed, the computer promptly stores the new balance in the data base so that the next credit check—even one made within minutes—will be based on up-to-date information.

and software designs that had been developed at great expense for batch processing. For the most part, OLTP capability was grafted onto such systems, as IBM had done with its successful CICS and IMS on-line software *(pages 46-47)*. As long as conventional batch systems could be employed in that fashion for OLTP—and modified if need be for backup capability—there was little incentive for the giants of the industry to embark on costly research-and-development efforts to create something new.

But in Jim Treybig's view, OLTP users were ready for a computer-age better mousetrap: a ready-made, economically-priced computer system with built-in backup capability. In 1973, after five years at Hewlett-Packard, Jimmy T. concluded that the time had come for him to go into business for himself.

BIRTH OF A COMPUTER COMPANY

To raise money, Treybig approached Thomas Perkins, the man who had hired him at HP. Perkins had since resigned as general manager of the company's computer division to form a venture-capital firm that specialized in funding high-tech start-ups. Treybig presented his former boss with the idea for developing an OLTP system that would compete in price and offer superior performance to the other systems then on the market.

Treybig's scheme testified to his willingness to take risks. Not only did the plan hinge on developing a new type of computer system, but Treybig's idea would place him in direct competition against the industry giant IBM, the dominant supplier of on-line processing systems. In 1974, common wisdom suggested that Treybig's position would be an uncomfortable one indeed. "Some of the major media said there'd never be another computer company—ever," said Treybig many years later in his distinctive East Texas drawl. One editorial cartoon of the era, he recalled, had summed up the situation with a sketch of a giant shark labeled IBM "swimming along, eating all the other computer companies."

But Perkins and his partner, Eugene Kleiner, a founder of Fairchild Semiconductor, one of the Valley's pioneering microchip firms, had the technical acumen to see that Treybig's David-and-Goliath scheme was feasible, even though it would take careful planning for it to have any hope of realizing its potential. To give Treybig the time to work out his idea more fully, Kleiner and Perkins took him into their firm as a limited partner, providing him with office space and the money he needed to assemble a core team.

In the summer of 1974, Treybig used $50,000 from the venture-capital firm to enlist his first two Hewlett-Packard designers, Mike Green and Jim Katzman, both of whom had been key architects of the company's flagship computer, the HP 3000. While Katzman and Green began to map out the design for the new computer and its operating system, Treybig went to work with Jack Loustanou, another former HP executive, on the business plan.

Within a few months, the little group had drawn up a five-year plan for the new company, down to hiring goals and manufacturing timetables. The plan included Katzman and Green's preliminary design for a computer system that would embody three characteristics they considered crucial to an on-line transaction-processing system: fault tolerance, on-line repair, and modular expandability. In other words, the computer would continue to run despite the failure of any single component; it would operate while faulty CPUs, power supplies, input/output controllers, or other elements were being repaired or replaced; and it would not even stop while new hardware components or application programs were added or substituted for old ones. On the strength of the plan, Kleiner-Perkins promptly put up a million dollars in seed money, and by autumn, Treybig was in business.

The only thing his company lacked was a name. Over the preceding months, a number of possibilities had been kicked around. Suggestions ranged from the brightly catchy—Dandi Data—to the soberly descriptive. Redundant Computers was a lumbering contender until someone pointed out that one meaning of "redundant" was "unnecessary." To help settle the issue, the group drew up a list, rotating a new name to the top each day to see how they liked the sound. At the end of November 1974, Loustanou got a call from the California Securities Commission asking how to record the still unnamed firm on the incorporation papers. The name crowning the list that day was Tandem, and thus was Tandem Computers christened.

A SYSTEM BUILT FROM THE GROUND UP

Searching out economical offices for the new corporation, Treybig's group moved in with another company backed by Kleiner-Perkins, a laser manufacturer with space to spare on its plant floor. A corner of the facility was partitioned off, and there the fledgling firm set up shop. As one early staffer later put it, abandoning giant Hewlett-Packard for those modest surroundings was "like jumping off the Queen Mary into a lifeboat."

But Tandem could offer its staff something that few established computer companies could match—the opportunity to take part in the creation of an entirely new computer. One of the earliest ideas for a Tandem OLTP system had been to modify equipment built by an established manufacturer and package it with a special proprietary operating system. But as Katzman and Green worked on the necessary integration, it became apparent to them that even with a custom operating system and any manner of ingenious hardware modifications, no available off-the-shelf computer had the necessary qualities to meet all three of their essential characteristics of a fault-tolerant computer capable of on-line transaction processing. Their solution was to build a computer from scratch.

To be certain that the system would turn out as envisioned, Tandem decided to design the hardware and software together. Doing so was a sharp departure from the usual practice in computer engineering—to build a new machine first, then to write an operating system for it. The prospect of taking part in such an adventure galvanized the technical staff. Dennis McEvoy, a member of the team that created the operating system and later Tandem vice president of software development, described the situation as "every software designer's dream—to build a system from the ground up."

The staff bent to the task with gusto. Treybig, who was as determined to build an enthusiastic and upbeat corporation as he was to storm the market with a new computer, lustily cheered them on. The company's motto was "Success through teamwork," and its founder did everything he could to foster an atmosphere that was conducive to both.

From the beginning, Tandem was run as openhandedly as any profit-driven company could be. Certificates of appreciation—hand-drawn and signed by Treybig himself—were accompanied by more tangible rewards, such as generous annual stock options awarded to all employees regardless of rank. Treybig refused to install time clocks and eschewed regular meetings, preferring to wander around the shop floor for impromptu conferences with his staff. Friday afternoon beer busts (politely called popcorn parties) became a permanent fixture at Tandem—a custom heartily endorsed by the president, who not only enjoyed a cold brew himself, but whose management style hinged on such unstructured communications.

The technical staff—many of them handpicked by Green and Katzman from among Hewlett-Packard's brightest young engineers and programmers—regularly worked sixty-hour weeks, crowded into open bullpens. Laboring equally long hours, Treybig and the firm's other executives ran the company from spartan offices that were furnished with plain black metal file cabinets and desks with fake wooden tops. From time to time, the president would be run out of his quarters to make room for an associate who needed a place to cogitate undisturbed.

The computer that took shape in this atmosphere of intense dedication and happy camaraderie that permeated Treybig's corner of the laser factory was given the working name Tandem-16. It was to contain between two and sixteen independent processing modules. If one unit failed for any reason, its work would be automatically shunted to one of its neighbors. Each module was, in essence, a separate computer with its own CPU, its own memory and its own operating system. The Tandem-16 was designed so that the processing load could be economically spread among several modules. The configuration lent itself well to on-line transaction processing, in which multiple transactions characteristically enter a system simultaneously, or nearly so.

Typically the computer would be set up so that each processor module was loaded with a different application program. For example, in a hotel-reservation system using a two-unit Tandem computer, one processor might be programmed to handle all requests for information about the number of available rooms, while another ran the software for making and canceling reservations. To ensure that one module could take over smoothly from the other in the event of a failure, the units were organized in a kind of buddy system. Each processor had a duplicate, passive copy of the other's application program tucked into a corner of its own memory.

The processors were connected to one another with a pair of high-speed data buses. Before performing any critical activity, such as updating the reservations data base, the processor preparing to perform that function would send the other processor what Tandem engineers dubbed a "checkpoint message." This contained the data and all the information that the backup processor would need in order to complete the transaction if there were a failure in the first unit.

In addition to checkpoint messages, the two processors sent each other a steady stream of communiqués regarding a host of cooperative activities. For example, if one module needed a piece of information that was under the other's control, the first processor would request the data by transmitting a message to the second, which responded by sending the information in a return message. If there were no such communications between the two processors for a period of one second, they exchanged simple messages to reassure one another that each was still functioning normally. These signals were called "I'm alive" messages.

If a processor broke down or became crippled for any reason, it stopped sending messages. Its buddy immediately assumed it to be in trouble, dropped it from the system, and automatically took over its work. At the same time, a message was sent to a printer or video terminal to notify the computer operator which component had failed. With the faulty element automatically switched out of the system, it could be replaced and the substitute brought on line with no interruption in service.

The regular drumbeat of communication between processing units was maintained by the operating system, called the Tandem/Transaction Operating System, or T/TOS. The ability to send and receive messages was at the heart of T/TOS—a copy of which was lodged in each processor module—and was the key to the Tandem system's fault-tolerant capability.

The operating system's ceaseless watchdog activity, which the engineers dubbed "paranoid democracy" because the units were created equal and maintained a suspicious eye on one another's activities, represented a degree of emergency preparedness that was unmatched in the commercial computer world. "We had to assume that anything that can go wrong, will," said McEvoy. "It was really a leap."

There was great urgency driving the work. "We had only a certain amount of time to get out the system," the software designer recalled, "or we'd run out of money." McEvoy later conceded that had he and his colleagues recognized the dimensions of the project, they might never have summoned the nerve to attempt it. Luckily, he said, "we didn't know enough to know we couldn't do it, so we took it on."

A BANK BUYS FIRST

Just seventeen months after they began, the job was done. In December 1975, the Tandem-16 was announced in a short *Business Week* story, headlined "A Computer That Won't Shut Down." The first machine was shipped to a customer, Citibank of New York, in May of the following year.

By that time, Tandem had renamed its machine the NonStop System, a term coined by marketing vice-president Sam Wiegand, who reasoned that his corporate customers would relate in a positive way to the concept of uninterruptable performance. Later, T/TOS also acquired a snappier, more commercially appealing moniker: the Guardian Operating System.

For on-line transaction processing, where there was no margin for error, no time for failure and recovery, the Tandem team believed it had devised the ultimate solution. Not only could their NonStop computer recover from the demise of any component, but it operated at extraordinarily high efficiency in the absence of failure. Unlike switched backup systems, in which the spare units contribute nothing unless pressed into service to replace the primary unit, the NonStop computer had no wastefully idle processors. Depending on how many modules were in the system, it could accomplish two to sixteen times the work of a single computer. And the modular configuration was ideal for expansion. Customers with modest processing needs could start out with a two-unit computer, then, as their requirements grew, add modules without the need to rewrite software or ever to shut down the system.

NEW DIRECTIONS IN BANKING

Tandem saw banks as potential customers who stood to benefit most from purchasing the NonStop System. When the new machine appeared, the banking industry already had nearly two decades' experience in expanding operations through computers. Until the early 1950s, for example, personal checking accounts were generally considered an expensive luxury. Except for the wealthy and the moderately so, most people bought goods and paid their bills with cash or money orders. But as banks acquired computers, and gradually extended their batch-processing capacity to include an increasing proportion of their accounting activities, the ability of these institutions to handle large numbers of checks increased—and the cost of doing so declined. Partly as a consequence, bankers were able to encourage customers lower on the economic ladder to open checking accounts. Between the 1950s and the mid-1970s, the portion of American households using this service ballooned from less than 30 percent to more than 90 percent.

Having attracted that additional business, banks were obliged to support it with expanded networks of branch banks. However, brick-and-mortar branches and the tellers to staff them are expensive, and bankers were determined to supplement them in routine transactions—deposits, withdrawals, account queries, and the like—with something less costly. One solution was to put computer terminals into the hands of customers. Thus was born the idea for the automatic teller machine (ATM).

The first ATMs were installed in the late 1960s. They functioned as standalone cash dispensers. Although each incorporated a small computer, none of them was connected to the bank's mainframe. An ATM read the magnetic stripe on a plastic card for such information as a customer's identification number and a preset withdrawal limit—say, fifty or one hundred dollars a day. Typically, when someone withdrew cash through an ATM, the machine recorded the transaction on the card's magnetic stripe so that another ATM, after reading the information, would not violate the customer's daily limit. The transaction was also recorded on tape inside the computer. This electronic journal, not unlike a tally sheet produced by a human clerk, would later be carried to a bank's central batch-processing computer where it would be used for updating customers' accounts.

A good idea in principle turned out to be less than perfect in practice. Early ATMs were plagued with mechanical difficulties and frequently malfunctioned. Less-than-perfect performance convinced many bank patrons that they were justified in preferring a face-to-face transaction with a live teller. Equally alienating to many customers were inflexible withdrawal limits that the ATM faithfully obeyed, regardless of the balance on account. As might be expected, bank customers tended to use the machines sporadically, as emergency cash dispensers, and the equipment did little to entice routine personal bank business away from tellers. To accomplish that goal, ATMs would have to become more reliable and offer better service.

The key to improved relations between ATMs and bank customers lay in OLTP systems, in which an ATM would tap into a bank's central data base of information about customers' checking and savings accounts and update the data each time a transaction took place. Customers would no longer be saddled with inconveniently low limits on their withdrawals, and they could ask the ATM for an account balance so that they could check, for example, whether a deposit had been credited.

Most banks, however, were reluctant to take this step. In the banks' view, their computers were too unreliable for consistent on-line performance. If one of the machines were to stumble for even a few seconds during an ATM transaction, the resulting confusion about the account in question could harm a bank's valued image of solidity and trustworthiness. What banks needed was a computer of unassailable reliability that could work around the clock—and Tandem had just the machine.

ELECTRONIC BANKING COMES OF AGE

Initially, however, the pioneer of fault-tolerant computing got the cold shoulder from bankers. Data-processing personnel at most large financial institutions in the United States had cut their teeth on IBM mainframe computers and had learned their programming skills at IBM-sponsored schools. Said Liam Carmody, in charge of retail products and services at First National State Bank of New Jersey when the NonStop System was introduced: "The love affair with IBM, common to many industries, was particularly intense in the banking industry." It took a great leap of faith, noted Carmody, for bankers even to consider a computer that was not made by IBM. Indeed, some of the earliest banks to buy the newcomer did not use it for banking at all. Citibank, Tandem's first customer, assigned its NonStop System to run a computerized phone directory—a large data base containing the names and extension numbers of the company's employees. Carmody's own bank, urged on by a younger generation of data-processing personnel who were not wedded to IBM, bought one for its new credit-card operation—an on-line system in which credit authorization terminals installed in retail stores were connected to a NonStop System at the bank's data-processing center.

Perhaps the most potent argument in selling the new service to merchants was the promise that the computer connected to a store's credit-authorization terminals would keep running full time. Moreover, not only did the computer's performance on the job fulfill its promise to store owners, but the machine's reliability also endeared it to data-processing personnel at the bank's main office. At the same time, other banks that were bold enough to experiment with Tandem computers for ATM systems were similarly taken with the machines, and the new computer's reputation started to grow. As Carmody later said, once banks had tried the system and learned that they could depend on it, they became fast converts. "Those little kinds of successes, here and there, chipped away at the initial resistance, and people became married to the idea and the concept."

In 1977, First National Bank of Chicago chose Tandem computers for a network to link the bank's headquarters with offices in twenty-four countries. Other sales to large banking institutions followed, and by the end of the decade Tandem was a major supplier to the banking industry. Continuous processing from Tandem had become the acknowledged standard for dependability in on-line electronic banking.

In response, other suppliers of computer systems to banks began vigorously exploring ways to enhance the reliability of their own machines. For the most part, Tandem's rivals applied their efforts to tailoring conventional mainframes for more trustworthy on-line use. They did this in part by taking advantage of advanced electronic technology; during the late 1970s, as microelectronic components evolved, computer hardware in general became increasingly less prone to failure.

None of the improved computers were fault-tolerant in the sense that Tandem computers were. In other words, they could not continue processing in the face of hardware or software failures and thus did not remove the need for a backup system. However, they became what is sometimes characterized as "highly available," meaning that the computers could be expected to break down infrequently and that they could be restored to action speedily if anything did go wrong. To protect data, new techniques were devised to copy it safely to a magnetic disk as information was entered into an on-line system, thus establishing audit trails that would allow information to be recovered if a computer failed partway through a transaction.

Thanks to more dependable computers, ATMs were no longer just a novelty; for customers who had discovered the speed and convenience of banking at a time and place of their choice, the machines had become a necessity. Supermarkets and service stations installed ATMs, becoming, in effect, branches of the banks in their areas. According to some estimates, by the mid-1980s, nearly 40 percent of bank customers nationwide were using ATMs for more than half their banking transactions, regularly stepping up to the machines to deposit funds, withdraw cash, make payments to credit-card accounts, and transfer money from one account to another. Within the industry there was no clear indication that ATMs actually reduced bankers' costs, but bankers readily acknowledged that the technology revolutionized the way American consumers handled their personal banking.

FILLING NEW NICHES

At the time that Tandem machines were leaving their mark on banking, they were making a similarly strong showing in other segments of the business world. Tandem systems were put to use across the full gamut of securities-business operations: managing stock-exchange tickers and feeding the latest quotes to dealers; storing client data and portfolio-analysis files; operating back-office record-keeping functions; maintaining securities-information data bases for stock exchanges and brokers; and networking to link brokers and exchanges together.

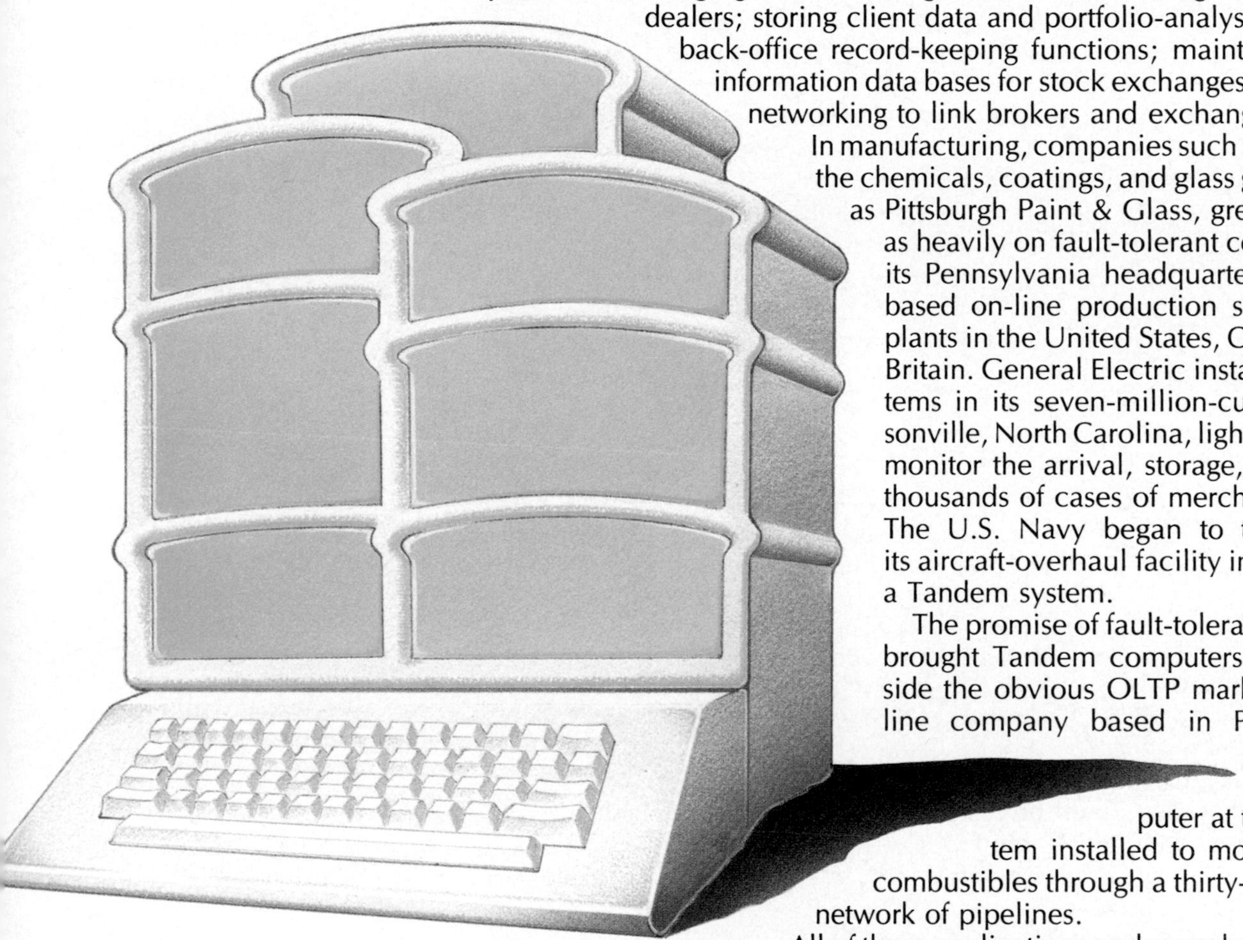

In manufacturing, companies such as PPG Industries, the chemicals, coatings, and glass giant once known as Pittsburgh Paint & Glass, grew to depend just as heavily on fault-tolerant computing, linking its Pennsylvania headquarters with Tandem-based on-line production systems at eleven plants in the United States, Canada, and Great Britain. General Electric installed Tandem systems in its seven-million-cubic-foot Hendersonville, North Carolina, lighting warehouse to monitor the arrival, storage, and shipment of thousands of cases of merchandise each day. The U.S. Navy began to track matériel at its aircraft-overhaul facility in San Diego using a Tandem system.

The promise of fault-tolerant operation even brought Tandem computers into realms outside the obvious OLTP markets. A fuel pipeline company based in Pennsylvania, for example, placed a NonStop computer at the heart of a system installed to monitor the flow of combustibles through a thirty-six-hundred-mile network of pipelines.

All of these applications and more had been predicted in the Tandem business plan drawn up in 1976. As Treybig later said: "We knew there was a market for a fault-tolerant system. There was no doubt. We only had to build it." But while Treybig had always been confident of success, perhaps even he could not have predicted how complete that success would be.

In 1980, Tandem Computers was ranked the fastest-growing public company in America. Its customer list, which numbered six in 1977, had expanded to 758 by 1983, with a total of 6,397 processor modules installed. Over the same six-year period, company revenues went from virtually nothing to $450 million. By 1984, Tandem had made the Fortune 500 list of the country's largest businesses, and customer loyalty was judged the highest in the computer industry, above even that of IBM. In less than ten years, the hopeful little start-up company had become one of the world's leading computer makers—a business success story impressive even by Silicon Valley standards.

Within the computer industry, Tandem was no less fabled for its distinctive corporate culture. As the company grew—eventually occupying five manufacturing plants and more than 100 branch offices around the globe—the esprit forged in the days of informal get-togethers and impromptu shop-floor chats with the boss was maintained through gatherings around a company swimming pool and basketball court. The weekly beer blasts continued, as did the freewheeling give-and-take among the staff, which kept in touch by means of a global electronic mail system.

In both its success and its laid-back style, Tandem Computers became one of the most prominent denizens of Silicon Valley, seeming to embody both the staggering riches to be reaped from the computer revolution and the new management style evolving in California's computer industry. But Tandem also symbolized something more far-reaching: the effect that a good idea, executed through well-thought-out technology, can have on people's lives.

The advent of computer systems that could be operated indefinitely without malfunctioning changed forever the way companies that owned them did business. Banks, given the ability to record every deposit or withdrawal as it took place, dramatically reduced the amount of paper they processed, allowing money to be transferred effortlessly by wire across continents or oceans. Factories began fine-tuning their output to meet demand, eliminating costly excess inventories of goods. Stock exchanges were able to keep up with an accelerated pace of trading that would have overwhelmed their earlier, manual approach to record keeping. The computer, which had once been a time- and labor-saving tool, had become the central nervous system for commerce in the United States and throughout much of the world. The aptly named Information Age had indeed arrived.

Electronic Banking

3

Computer technology has substantially changed the ways in which governments, corporations, and even individuals take care of their financial affairs. With computers has come electronic banking, for example, a new style for a venerable business. Computers have speeded up many traditional banking services and spawned new ones unimaginable when the tools of the industry were the typewriter and the adding machine. Today, money, and information about money, can be moved from place to place much faster and more accurately than in the past. As an extra dividend, computers dramatically reduce the volume of paper—checks, receipts, and other records of transactions—that banks must process.

Electronic banking appeals to customers as well. Corporate customers can whisk money by wire from one city or country to another, consummating in hours or minutes deals that would once have taken days or weeks to complete. And individuals can benefit in a variety of ways.Through automated teller machines (ATMs), they have access to their accounts any time they like. An ordinary push-button telephone becomes a means to pay bills without writing checks. And many individuals elect to receive an electronic paycheck in lieu of a paper one, saving a trip to the bank every payday and circumventing the "float," a post-deposit period when the money may not be available for use.

As explained on the following pages, the brave new world of electronic banking has been created largely by on-line transaction processing, the ability of a bank's computer to continuously update its records so that every deposit, withdrawal, or other transaction is recorded at the moment it takes place. By harnessing this on-line processing power, banks have been able to streamline their own operations even as they provide the marketplace with a range of new services.

The Electronic Paycheck

To issue electronic paychecks, companies send to their respective banks a computer payroll tape containing payment records for the employees who have chosen direct deposit. Each record includes the identification number of the employee's bank, the employee's bank-account number, and the amount of the payment. A paper record of the amount of payment and any sums withheld is sent separately to the employee.

Millions of workers in the United States collect their salaries without ever touching paychecks. They do so through direct deposit, an electronic-banking technique in which money is transferred from company to employee by deducting a sum from one computer file and adding it to another. Direct deposit, which greatly reduces paperwork and also frees the employee from worry about lost or stolen checks, is made possible by a computerized financial facility known as an automated clearinghouse.

A traditional clearinghouse receives checks that have been deposited at many different financial institutions and calcu-

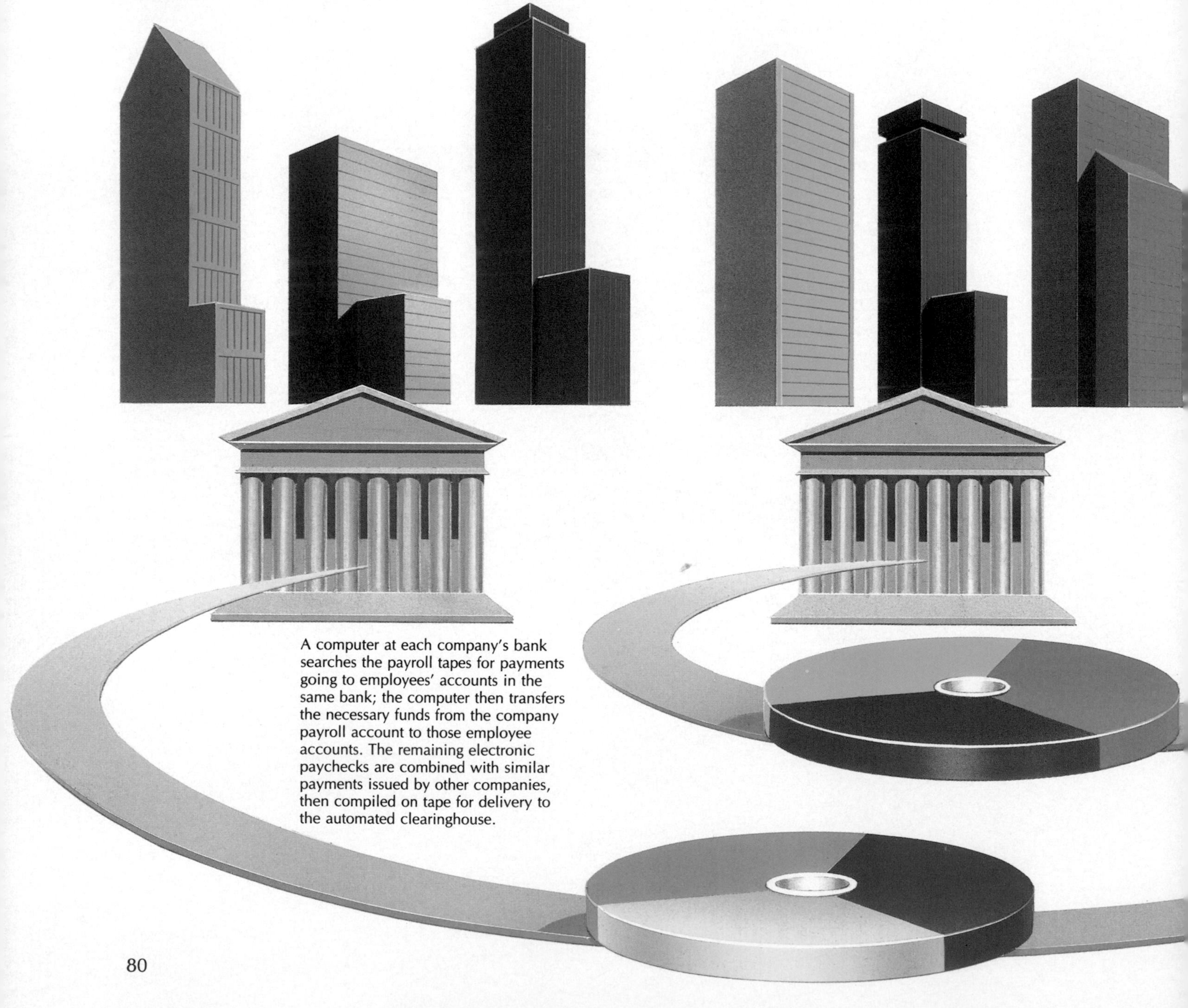

A computer at each company's bank searches the payroll tapes for payments going to employees' accounts in the same bank; the computer then transfers the necessary funds from the company payroll account to those employee accounts. The remaining electronic paychecks are combined with similar payments issued by other companies, then compiled on tape for delivery to the automated clearinghouse.

lates the amount that is to be credited to each one. At the same time, it calculates the amount to be deducted from the banks that have issued those checks. The clearinghouse then sorts all the checks and forwards them to their issuing banks so that the amounts can be deducted from the balances of the individuals—or institutions—who wrote those checks. By using a clearinghouse, a bank can do business with hundreds of other banks without having to deal separately with each one.

Many check clearinghouses in the United States are run by consortia of banks operating with the Federal Reserve. The Federal Reserve requires each private bank to maintain minimum monetary reserves; among other uses, these funds serve to settle accounts between the financial institutions as checks are processed through the clearinghouses.

With the advent of computer technology that could handle direct deposits, the Federal Reserve enhanced its clearinghouse system to process "electronic checks"—payment orders that are transferred from computer to computer along telephone lines or delivered on magnetic disks or tapes. Just as banks send paper checks to traditional clearinghouses, they can now send electronic checks to automated clearinghouses (ACHs) to be sorted and distributed by computer.

Payroll tapes arrive at the automated clearinghouse twice a day. Computers sort the electronic paychecks by receiving bank and prepare a separate tape for each bank to which payment is due.

Upon receiving a tape from the ACH, the bank's computer stores the data, then uses the employee account number accompanying each electronic payment record to distribute the money and to record the deposit on each customer's monthly bank statement.

Using a push-button phone, the customer calls the telephone banking service. Unlike the pulses generated by a rotary dial, which carry only as far as the local telephone exchange, the dual-tone frequencies of a push-button phone can transmit instructions through the telephone system to the bank's computer.

"WELCOME TO THE TELE-BANK SYSTEM. PLEASE ENTER YOUR ACCOUNT NUMBER."

The customer pushes the proper buttons on the telephone, pressing the pound sign (#) to signal when the sequence of numbers is complete.

Asked for an account number, the customer responds by entering a series of digits using the telephone keypad. The computer checks the response against a file of valid account numbers stored in memory. If the computer recognizes the customer's number, the transaction can proceed.

"ACCOUNT NUMBER 052104911. PLEASE ENTER YOUR PERSONAL IDENTIFICATION NUMBER."

The customer enters his PIN, a series of four or more digits, to confirm account ownership.

To protect the bank and its customers from fraud, personal identification numbers (PINs) are not stored in the computer, where they and their associated account numbers might fall prey to computer criminals. Instead, each PIN is associated with its account number by a third number, called an offset number. The process is such that calculating the PIN from the offset and account numbers is virtually impossible. Stored in the computer, the offset number helps to determine whether the customer's PIN is valid as entered. If so, the transaction continues.

"WHAT TYPE OF TRANSACTION WOULD YOU LIKE TO MAKE?"

Wishing to pay a bill, the customer enters the code for such a transaction.

A Machine That Talks

An ARU, in its role as the voice of a computer, uses human speech to hold up its end of a telephone conversation with a bank customer. To give such a machine speech, system designers specify all the responses that the ARU might be called upon to issue and examine them for words or combinations of words that they have in common—"Please enter your," for example, or "account number." Each response fragment, along with numbers for confirming transaction amounts and account numbers, is enunciated by a human voice and recorded on tape. It is then digitized—converted to strings of ones and zeros—and stored in the ARU's memory under a phrase code. Programmed with the phrase codes that constitute the appropriate response to any step of a telephone-banking transaction, the ARU summons the proper codes from memory and reconverts the ones and zeros into speech with a voice generator.

Paying Bills with a Telephone Call

Banks have long accepted payments on behalf of local utility companies, a service that saves bank customers the cost of mailing checks. And because the bank can combine into a single payment any number of checks made out to one company, the practice slightly reduces the flood of paper through the check-clearing apparatus.

Telephone banking goes a step further, saving the customer a trip to the bank and possibly eliminating checks altogether. A customer can also order a payment to be made at a later date, a feature that keeps bills from becoming overdue because of a vacation or an extended business trip. In place of a canceled check, a line in the customer's monthly statement describing the payment proves that payment was made.

The device that makes telephone banking possible is called an audio-response unit, or ARU, which links the customer's telephone to the bank computer. The ARU includes a voice generator *(below, left)* that enables it to respond to the customer's actions during a transaction *(opposite, bottom)*. In the bill-paying conversation running diagonally across these pages, statements in quotation marks represent how the ARU's voice might prompt the customer each step of the way. By pressing the appropriate keys on the telephone, the customer can backtrack to the previous step to correct any error made in entering an account number or other information.

"PLEASE ENTER PAYEE CODE."

The customer enters a number that instructs the computer whom to credit with the funds, a utility company perhaps.

"PAYEE CODE 4913. PLEASE ENTER PAYMENT AMOUNT."

The customer enters the amount he wishes to pay on the bill.

"YOU HAVE ENTERED $25.00. PLEASE ENTER PAYEE CODE."

With no additional bills to pay, the customer instead presses the appropriate code to end the bill-payment transaction.

When the customer concludes the bill-paying session, the computer compares the total paid out with the balance in the customer's account. In the event that the payments requested would result in an overdrawn account, some computers give the customer an opportunity to pay smaller amounts.

"YOU HAVE PAID $25.00 FOR BILL PAYMENT. THANK YOU. WHAT TYPE OF TRANSACTION WOULD YOU LIKE TO MAKE?"

The customer, having completed his banking, enters a code to end the call.

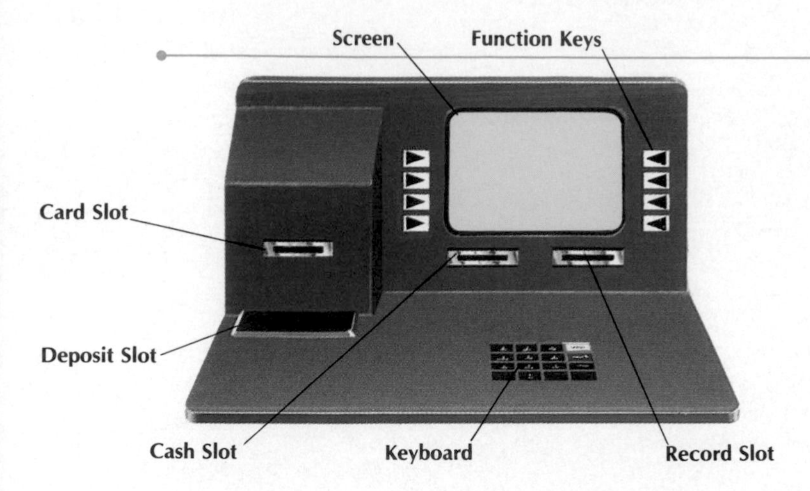

A Computerized Bank Teller

Nearly half of all bank customers in the United States have used an automated teller machine, or ATM, at one time or another. This device, essentially a small computer system in disguise, lets bank customers avoid long teller lines and take care of common transactions—make deposits and withdrawals, and transfer money between accounts, among others—at their own convenience, seven days a week.

ATMs are popular with banks; compared with the person-

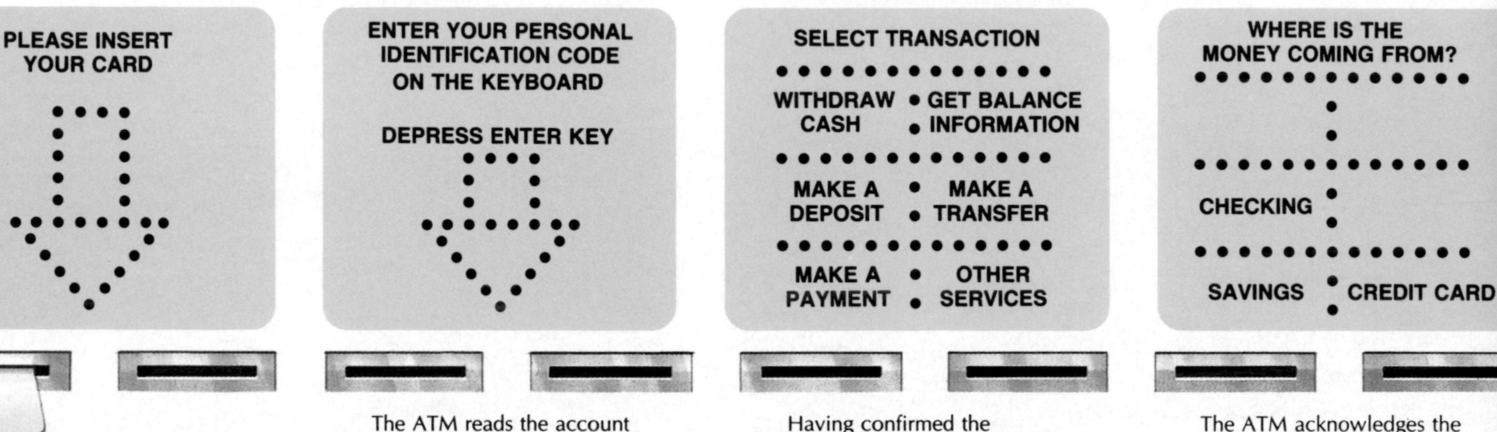

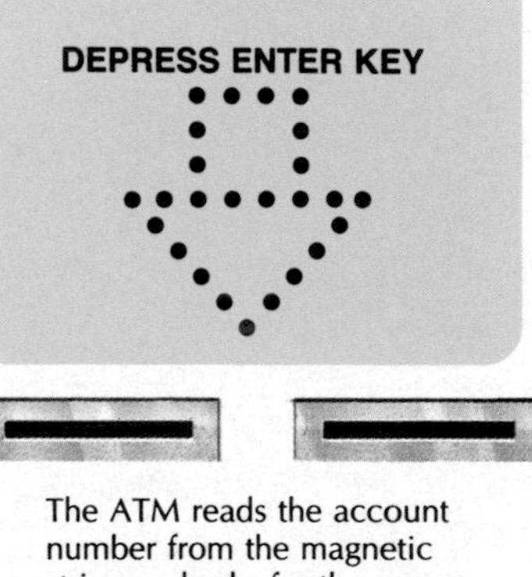

The customer slides an ATM card into the machine's card slot. Sensors behind the opening check that the card has been inserted with the magnetic stripe in the correct position. If so, rollers advance the card to the machine's card reader.

The ATM reads the account number from the magnetic stripe and asks for the customer's personal identification number (PIN). As in the bank-by-phone system, the machine keeps no record of the PIN, but verifies it through an intricate mathematical calculation.

Having confirmed the customer's account number and PIN, the ATM grants access to its computerized banking services, offering a menu of possible transactions. The customer elects to withdraw some cash.

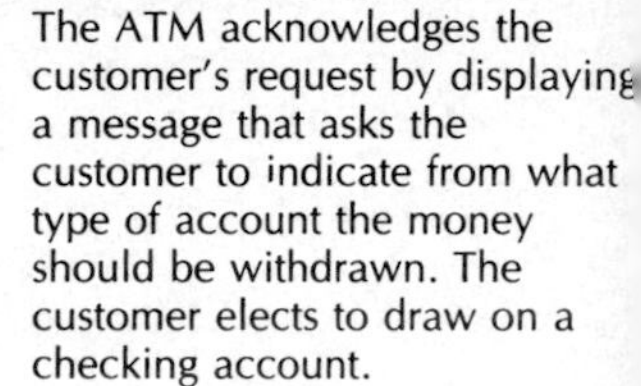

The ATM acknowledges the customer's request by displaying a message that asks the customer to indicate from what type of account the money should be withdrawn. The customer elects to draw on a checking account.

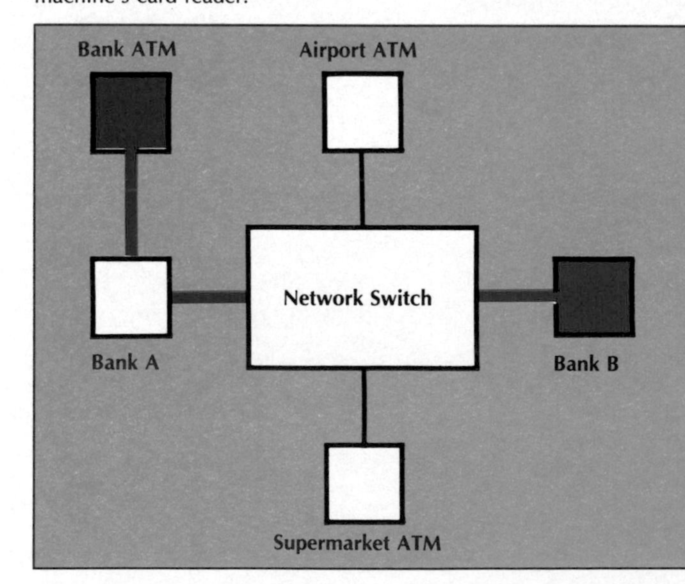

Multibank ATM Networks

To permit an ATM of one bank to converse with the host computer of another, each ATM is connected to a network switch either directly or indirectly, through a bank. In either case, the ATM transmits a bank-identity number, read from the magnetic stripe on an ATM card, to the switch. Based on this information, the switch routes the transaction to the appropriate bank's host computer. In the transaction at left, a customer of Bank B initiates a cash withdrawal from an ATM belonging to Bank A *(far left)*. Bank A relays the request to the switch, which stores the message for later use in settling accounts between banks and forwards it to Bank B. After approving the transaction, Bank B notifies the network switch, which instructs Bank A's ATM to dispense the cash.

nel cost of handling a high volume of transactions, the machines are economical. In addition, ATMs can be installed almost anywhere—in shopping malls, supermarkets, airports—permitting banks to improve customer service without incurring the expense of full-fledged branch offices.

There are two varieties of ATMs: on-line and off-line. Each on-line machine in a bank's network of ATMs is linked directly to the bank's central computer by way of a telephone line. An off-line machine, on the other hand, is an isolated outpost; it is not connected to the bank's central computer: it does all computation on its own.

Off-line ATMs can pose security risks. Because the off-line ATM does not enjoy access to account-balance information, a customer might be able to withdraw more cash than his account contains. Such an occurrence would be unlikely with on-line machines, which can update an account balance in the central computer after each transaction. An added advantage of on-line ATMs is that groups of banks can share ATM resources through a computer called a network switch *(box)*. With this arrangement, customers of one bank can use the ATMs of any other bank in the network.

A bank customer's key to an ATM is a plastic card with a magnetized stripe on the back recorded with account numbers and other pertinent information. The customer uses the card to activate the ATM and then, as shown in the cash-withdrawal transaction illustrated on these pages, communicates with the machine by pressing keys in response to messages that flash onto the ATM screen.

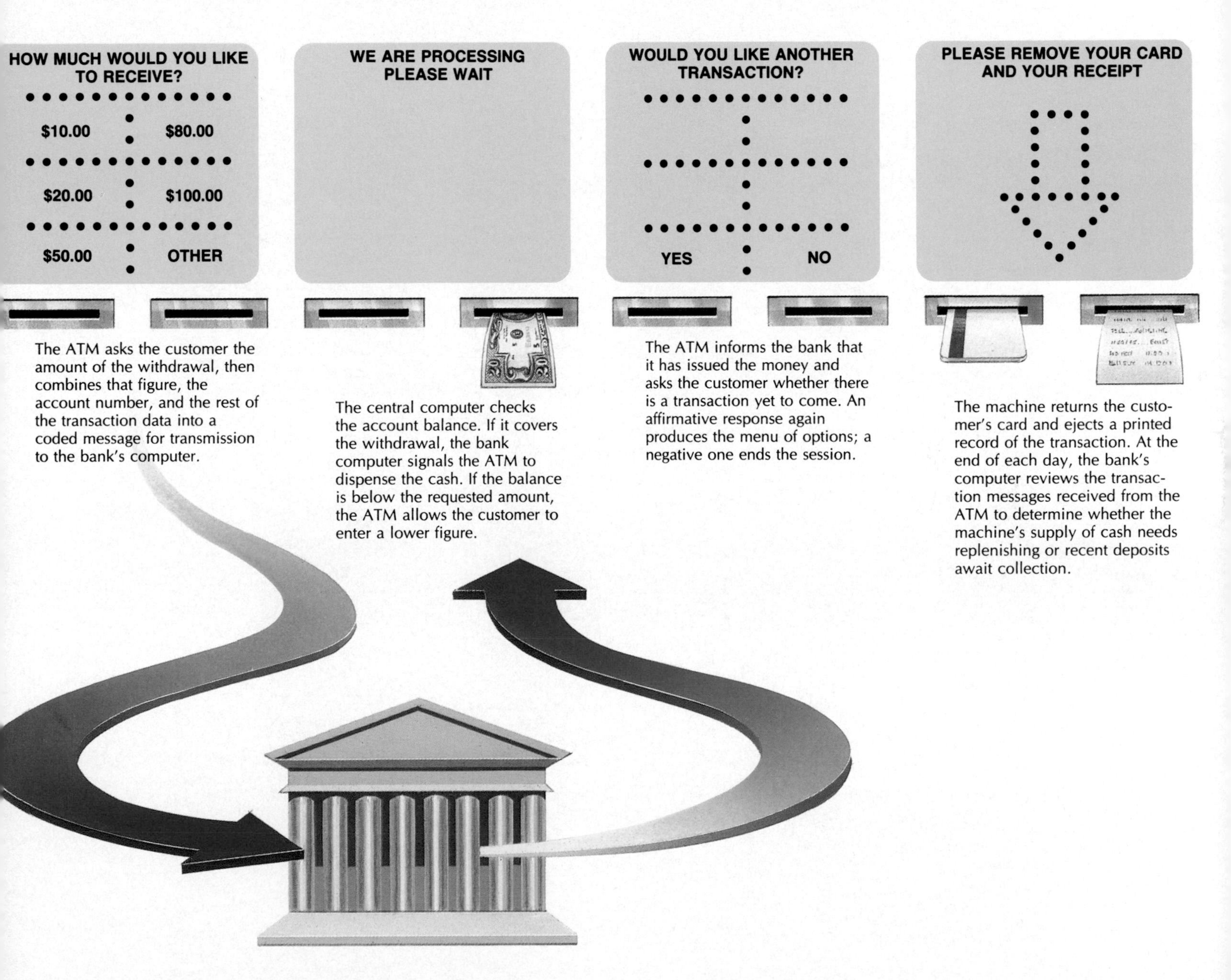

The ATM asks the customer the amount of the withdrawal, then combines that figure, the account number, and the rest of the transaction data into a coded message for transmission to the bank's computer.

The central computer checks the account balance. If it covers the withdrawal, the bank computer signals the ATM to dispense the cash. If the balance is below the requested amount, the ATM allows the customer to enter a lower figure.

The ATM informs the bank that it has issued the money and asks the customer whether there is a transaction yet to come. An affirmative response again produces the menu of options; a negative one ends the session.

The machine returns the customer's card and ejects a printed record of the transaction. At the end of each day, the bank's computer reviews the transaction messages received from the ATM to determine whether the machine's supply of cash needs replenishing or recent deposits await collection.

Moving Money by Computer

An art dealer in Washington, D.C., wishing to buy a painting from a gallery in France, visits his local bank, where he initiates a payment order to the French dealer.

Originating Bank

The Washington bank, the originating bank in this transaction, deducts the price of the painting from the dealer's account. The bank's computer then composes an encrypted funds-transfer message, a payment order crediting the receiving bank in Paris with the price of the painting.

Federal Reserve Bank

The computer at the originating bank transmits the funds-transfer order via Fedwire to the regional Federal Reserve Bank, where another computer logs in its data bank a debit against the originating bank's account. The Federal Reserve computer likewise credits the next bank in the chain of communication, the correspondent bank that provides a link between Fedwire and the S.W.I.F.T. international financial message network.

Correspondent Ban

After receiving the funds-transfer message, the correspondent bank rewrites the payment order in a format acceptable to S.W.I.F.T. It then sends the message to a S.W.I.F.T. computer, known as a concentrator, that handles communications with many banks in the same region.

S.W.I.F.T. Concentrator

The concentrator verifies that the correspondent bank is a network member and acknowledges the message. The concentrator encrypts the payment order and sends it to a S.W.I.F.T. computer—called a switch—for transmission overseas.

S.W.I.F.T. Switch

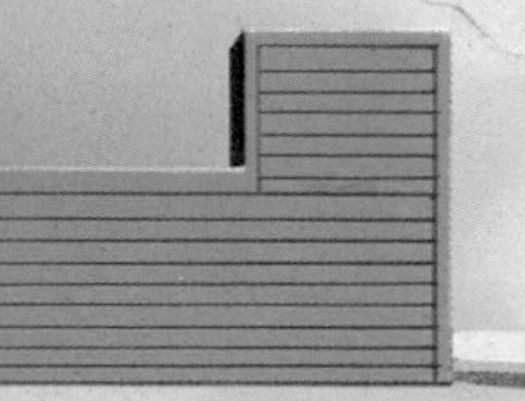

After entering the arrival of the message in a log and checking the format, the S.W.I.F.T. switch identifies the message's destination and looks up the relevant routing data in a set of tables stored in memory. Finally, the switch transmits the payment order to a S.W.I.F.T. switch in Europe by way of transatlantic telephone lines and satellite.

Until the early 1970s, widely separated banks did a great deal of business by telex, a communications system for sending typed messages over telephone lines. The practice had several disadvantages. It was slow, sometimes requiring more than an hour to prepare a message for transmission and a similar period to process it upon arrival. Instructions for international transactions faced language barriers that could cause errors, and messages often went astray.

Computerization of long-distance banking was the remedy. Standardized formats for transaction messages virtually eliminate misunderstandings. To transmit a message customarily requires no more than ten minutes. Messages are rarely lost. And computers can encrypt them to achieve a measure of confidentiality that was formerly unknown to interbank communications.

Several electronic-payment networks have been established. Fedwire, a prominent domestic network, links financial institutions to one another through the Federal Reserve. Other networks—S.W.I.F.T. (Society for Worldwide Interbank Financial Telecommunication) and CHIPS (Clearing House Interbank Payments System), for example—are owned by bank consortia. Electronic payments may pass through a number of banks and networks in the course of a transaction, as seen in the international example traced on these pages.

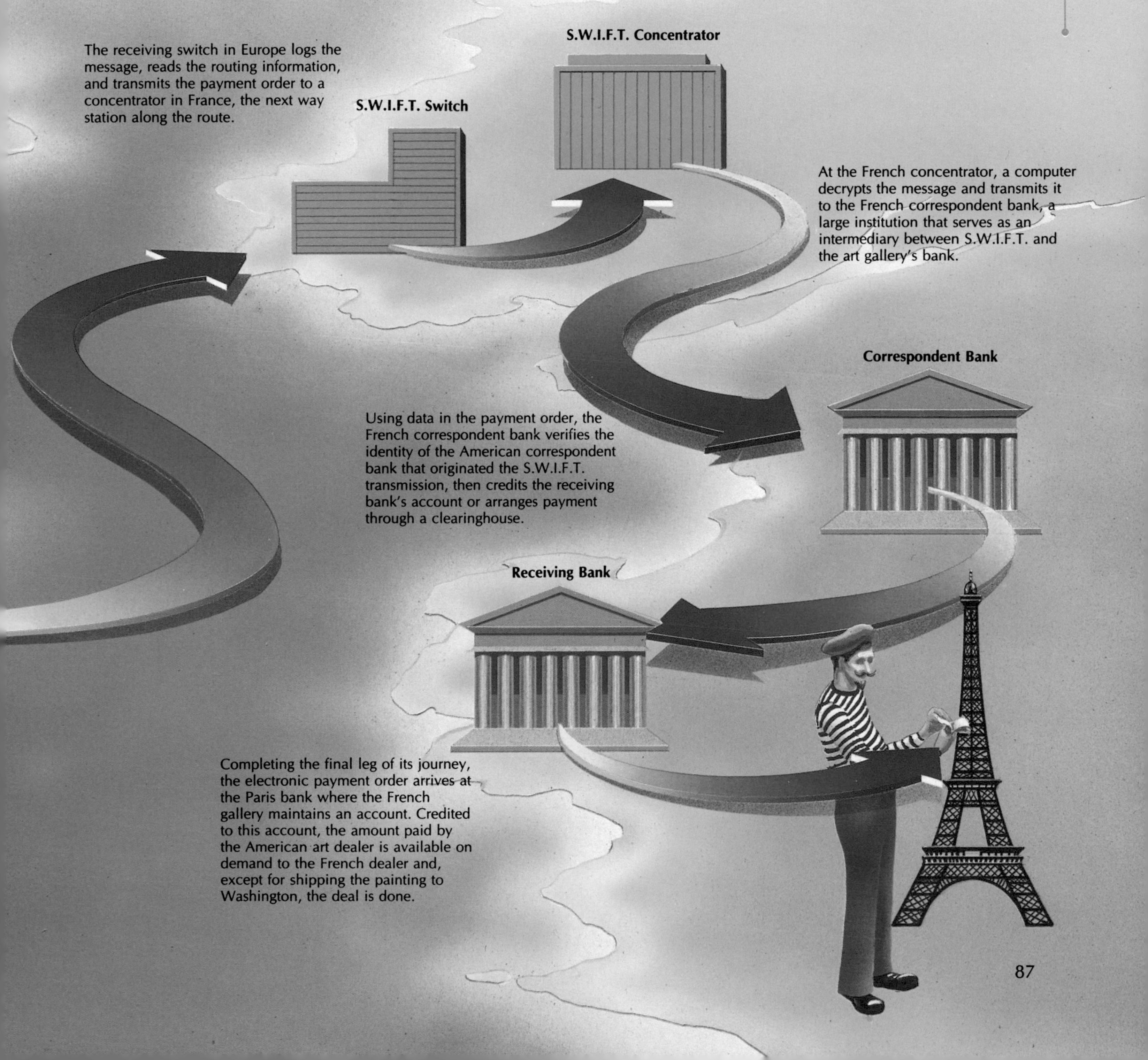

S.W.I.F.T. Switch

The receiving switch in Europe logs the message, reads the routing information, and transmits the payment order to a concentrator in France, the next way station along the route.

S.W.I.F.T. Concentrator

At the French concentrator, a computer decrypts the message and transmits it to the French correspondent bank, a large institution that serves as an intermediary between S.W.I.F.T. and the art gallery's bank.

Correspondent Bank

Using data in the payment order, the French correspondent bank verifies the identity of the American correspondent bank that originated the S.W.I.F.T. transmission, then credits the receiving bank's account or arranges payment through a clearinghouse.

Receiving Bank

Completing the final leg of its journey, the electronic payment order arrives at the Paris bank where the French gallery maintains an account. Credited to this account, the amount paid by the American art dealer is available on demand to the French dealer and, except for shipping the painting to Washington, the deal is done.

Invasion of the Microprocessors

4

In the summer of 1969, representatives from the Japanese firm Busicom, a manufacturer of electronic calculators, met in California with officials of the American firm Intel, maker of memory chips for mainframe computers. Busicom had decided to produce a new line of business and scientific calculators and approached Intel to supply the electronics that were the heart of such devices. Intel was at the leading edge of integrated-circuit technology, recently developed processes for fitting many hundreds of transistors, other electronic components, and the wires linking them onto small wafers of silicon.

Intel had just produced a breakthrough integrated circuit (IC) containing more than two thousand transistors. Busicom, realizing that this remarkable degree of miniaturization could be used not just for memory but for many other kinds of circuits, sought out Intel to build the ICs for their new calculators, and Intel agreed to take on the work. By the time the job was finished—and much to the surprise of everyone involved—the company had set the stage for the application of computers to activities so broad in scope, so varied in detail that only the most reckless of forecasters might have predicted the outcome. Intel engineers had invented the microprocessor, an integrated-circuit essence of computer—a CPU on a single chip.

At first, no one at Intel imagined that the microprocessor would become anything other than what it was designed to be—a convenient way to build a calculator. But within a decade, descendants of Intel's cleverly contrived device had worked their way into the fabric of society. Microprocessors were employed not only as logic engines for calculators, but as controllers of traffic lights. They appeared in household appliances—sewing machines, refrigerators, microwave ovens—that people used every day, turning almost everyone into unwitting computer operators.

Within twenty years of the microprocessor's invention, toys had acquired computers for brains, enabling a doll, for example, to respond to its own name or to ask for a sweater in the cool of the evening. Augmented by operating systems that in many respects evolved to levels of sophistication that rivaled their mainframe cousins, the microprocessor, along with other developments in computer hardware and software, made possible desktop computers more versatile and powerful than the largest mainframe on line when Intel produced the first microprocessor. No longer were computers solely the province of rich and powerful corporations. Anyone with as little as several hundred dollars could computerize a corner of society.

DAWN OF THE MICRO AGE

Well into the 1960s, calculators were mechanical devices that used the turning of gears to represent numbers—a single revolution of the ones gear was accompanied by a tenth of a revolution of the tens gear, a hundredth of a revolution of the hundreds gear, and so on. Produced by companies like Burroughs and

Singer, the sewing-machine company, these machines, even when operated by an electric motor, were slow at their calculations and, in the main, limited to the four most basic mathematical functions: addition, subtraction, multiplication, and division.

In 1961, the English firm Sumlock Comptometer Company, Ltd., brought out one of the first electronic calculators. This device, as well as those produced a short time later by Texas Instruments and other companies, used temporary memory and permanently wired logic circuits to replace the gears found in mechanical calculators. In the logic circuits were stored the rules or algorithms for performing mathematical operations—for example, instructions for adding two figures or for determining the square root of a number; to save space several such logic circuits might share a single chip. Temporary memory was used to store numbers entered by way of the keyboard, generated by the logic chips in the process of completing a calculation, or presented as a final answer for display. Designing such calculators entailed laying out a special set of integrated circuits for each one.

A TECHNOLOGY OVERWHELMED

Busicom approached Intel with plans for an entire line of calculators, each optimized for a specific purpose. Because of special features to be included (one was to have a built-in printer), each logic chip would require a larger number of transistors than had yet been assembled in a single integrated circuit. The earliest ICs had incorporated up to a dozen transistors. They had been followed by more densely packed circuits having hundreds of transistors. Intel had recently experimented with a technology that would allow the company to squeeze 2,000 transistors onto a chip. However, the complexity of Busicom's calculator designs would require chips containing 3,000 to 5,000 transistors each.

Intel assigned an innovative young designer named Marcian E. Hoff to the Busicom project. Known as Ted to his associates, Hoff soon concluded that Busicom's plans were too ambitious. Although Intel might be able to manufacture a few chips with the required number of transistors, Hoff feared that the success rate would be low, with many faulty ICs produced for each good one. The result would have been a prohibitively expensive chip.

But Ted Hoff had an idea: Instead of building a separate logic chip for each calculator function, he would design a general-purpose logic chip that could perform any of the operations called for. Hoff estimated that the circuitry would all fit on one IC of fewer than 2,000 transistors, well within Intel's capabilities. In effect, the chip would be a miniature version of the the central processing unit of large computers. For his invention, Hoff and his team coined the word microprocessor.

Besides reducing the number of transistors in each silicon wafer, Hoff's approach offered other advantages. Where a Busicom design might call for as many as a dozen of their exceedingly complex chips, the Intel proposal required only four—the microprocessor and three chips containing additional circuits to manage the calculator's memory and input/output devices such as the keyboard, the numerical display for answers, or a printer. Furthermore, the Intel chips would have only sixteen pins, or connectors, to a circuit board, where the

Busicom chips had forty, vastly complicating wiring inside the calculators. The smaller number of ICs and simpler wiring permitted the calculators to be designed more compactly.

Initially, Busicom's engineers were skeptical, but in late summer of 1969, they accepted Hoff's proposal as a much more flexible and economical approach than producing a separate set of ICs for each calculator. About a year later, in 1970, Intel unveiled the world's first microprocessor, an integrated circuit designated the 4004, a name that reflected the four-bit chunk, or word, of data that the chip handled. Shortly thereafter, Intel began producing it exclusively for the Japanese calculator maker.

The devices that Busicom and its competitors brought to market, although they were called calculators, were in essence special-purpose computers that took input from a keypad studded with number keys and keys labeled with mathematical functions, processed the information according to software that was wired permanently into electronic circuits, and displayed the result, or output, either as lighted numbers or as print on paper. No operating system existed for the microprocessor at this stage of its development, but it was little missed. The software for each function was written once, then mass-produced. These calculators were in reality a kind of appliance; as a toaster toasts bread, they solved a specific repertoire of mathematical problems. If it was a nuisance for the manufacturer to program every single step of the algorithm for solving a problem, from input to output, the inconvenience was inconsequential; once the program was written, it rarely had to be changed. Moreover, early calculators were not reprogrammable, so their owners had no need for an operating system.

COMPUTERS FOR THE HOMEMAKER

The use of microprocessors in electronic calculators was the prelude to the computerization of a vast array of everyday appliances. One of the first of these was the sewing machine. That the Singer Company manufactured mechanical calculators as well as sewing machines is not as odd as it may seem. Both devices were marvels of mechanical engineering and precision, the sewing machine containing a shaft with many cams, eccentrically shaped lobes that controlled the feed of the material forward or backward and moved the sewing-machine needle from side to side as necessary to sew a wide variety of construction stitches for holding garments together and decorative stitches to make them attractive.

About the time that Intel brought out the 4004 microprocessor, Donald Kircher, president of Singer, began to be intrigued with the possibility of somehow making the sewing machine electronic. To pursue that goal, he hired John Rydz as vice president for engineering. As an officer of Diebold, Inc., the safe and vault company, Rydz had been instrumental in developing the company's first automatic-teller machines. Kircher felt that Rydz had precisely the kind of experience—disguising a computer as an appliance—that Singer needed if the company was to advance beyond the exclusively mechanical sewing machines of the past.

To orient himself in his new job, Rydz took up sewing, spending many hours experimenting with Singer's top-of-the-line model, the Futura. Offering a choice

Anatomy of a Bar Code

A fitting emblem for the computerized society, bar codes appear on everything from railroad cars to cans of soup. They serve as computerized labels that allow information to be entered automatically into a computer system, speeding retail transactions and improving asset management in unprecedented fashion.

The symbol's dark bars and light spaces of varying width are a message written in the binary language of zeros and ones that computers understand. Any of several types of scanning device *(pages 104-107)* can read the message by sweeping a small beam of light across it; dark bars reflect less light than do the spaces, and the scanner picks up the variations, decoding the patterns into electrical signals for the computer.

Bar-code formats vary, but one of the most common is the Universal Product Code (UPC), used for labeling most grocery items and general merchandise. UPC symbols form a twelve-digit numerical code that identifies a specific product; the code is, in effect, an address for a data-base file where the computer can look up the item's current price and adjust its inventory count *(page 97)*.

As the example below illustrates, each decimal digit in a UPC symbol takes up two bars and two spaces, which themselves consist of a total of seven units, or modules, that stand for individual zeros and ones; a single bar or space may be anywhere from one to four modules wide. Border areas and control patterns account for the rest of the symbol's spaces and stripes. Other features of the UPC design are explained on the following pages.

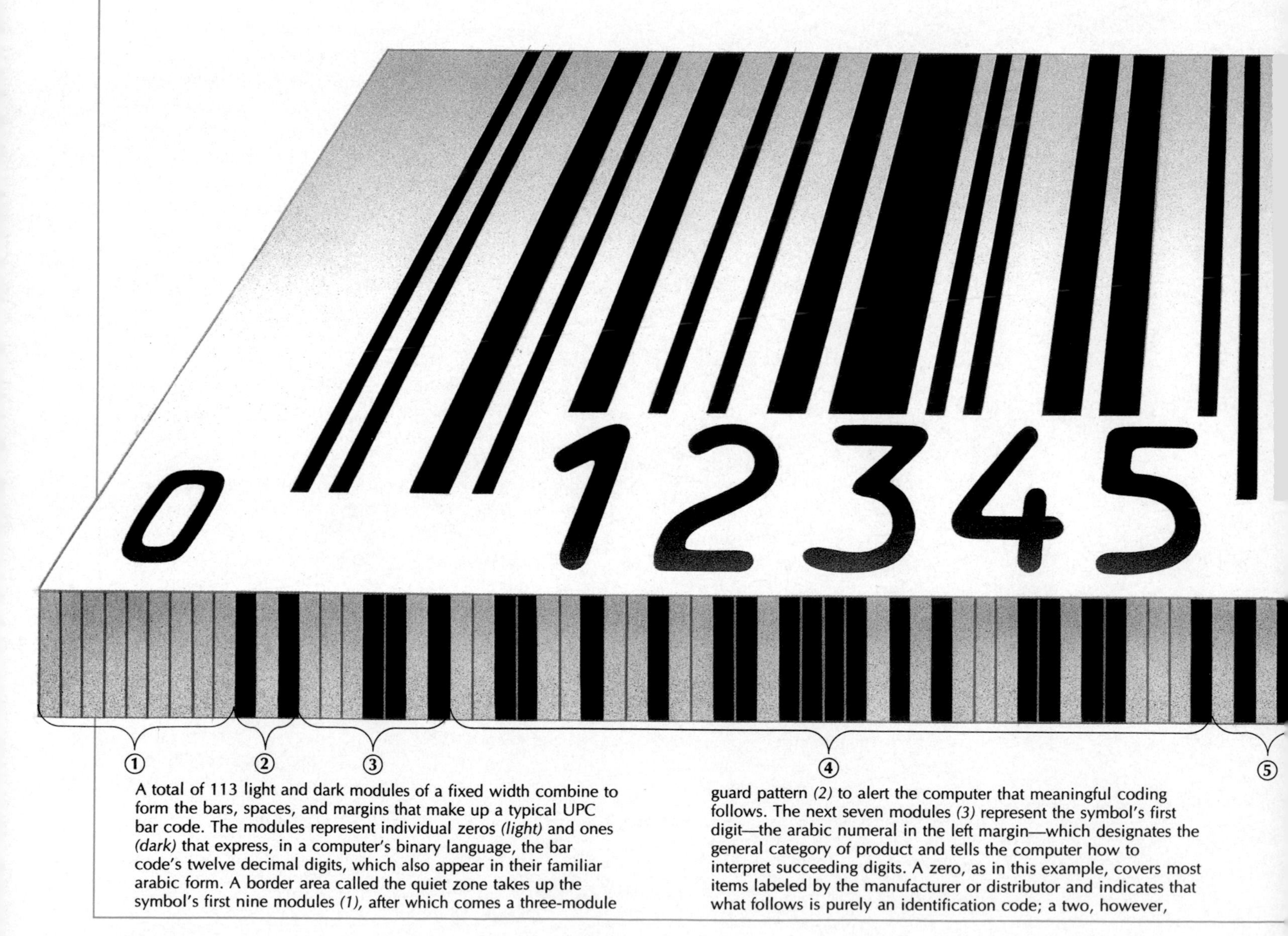

A total of 113 light and dark modules of a fixed width combine to form the bars, spaces, and margins that make up a typical UPC bar code. The modules represent individual zeros *(light)* and ones *(dark)* that express, in a computer's binary language, the bar code's twelve decimal digits, which also appear in their familiar arabic form. A border area called the quiet zone takes up the symbol's first nine modules *(1)*, after which comes a three-module guard pattern *(2)* to alert the computer that meaningful coding follows. The next seven modules *(3)* represent the symbol's first digit—the arabic numeral in the left margin—which designates the general category of product and tells the computer how to interpret succeeding digits. A zero, as in this example, covers most items labeled by the manufacturer or distributor and indicates that what follows is purely an identification code; a two, however,

A Recipe for Accuracy

The bar code's twelfth digit results from a series of calculations performed on the first eleven. When the symbol is scanned, the store computer checks for errors by repeating the calculations, as outlined below; if the result still matches the symbol's last digit, the code was read accurately.

- Add all the digits in odd positions: $0 + 2 + 4 + 1 + 7 + 9 = 23$
- Multiply the result by 3: $23 \times 3 = 69$
- Add all the digits in even positions: $1 + 3 + 5 + 6 + 8 = 23$
- Add the last two results: $69 + 23 = 92$
- Subtract the result from the next-highest multiple of 10 to yield the check digit: $100 - 92 = 8$

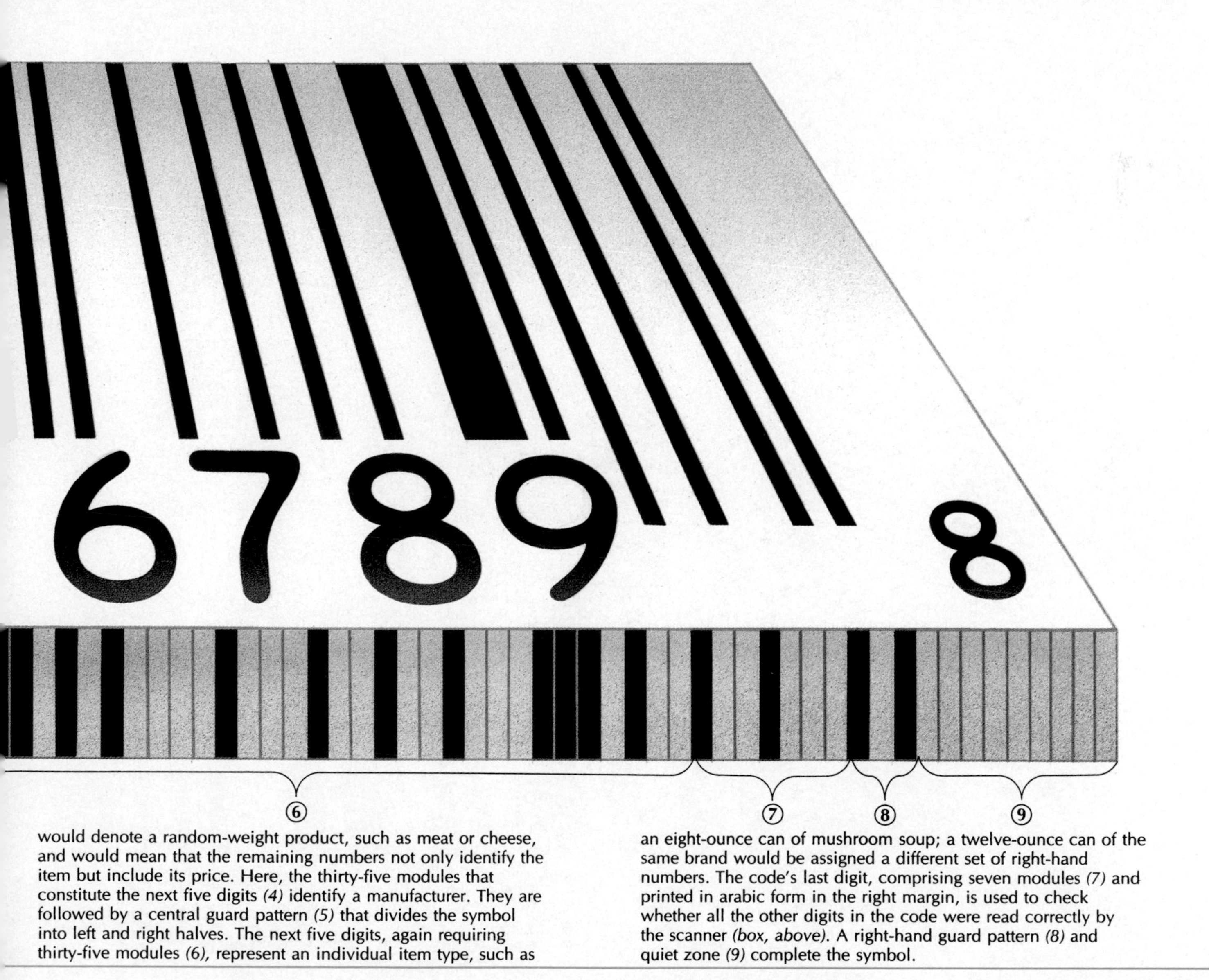

would denote a random-weight product, such as meat or cheese, and would mean that the remaining numbers not only identify the item but include its price. Here, the thirty-five modules that constitute the next five digits *(4)* identify a manufacturer. They are followed by a central guard pattern *(5)* that divides the symbol into left and right halves. The next five digits, again requiring thirty-five modules *(6)*, represent an individual item type, such as an eight-ounce can of mushroom soup; a twelve-ounce can of the same brand would be assigned a different set of right-hand numbers. The code's last digit, comprising seven modules *(7)* and printed in arabic form in the right margin, is used to check whether all the other digits in the code were read correctly by the scanner *(box, above)*. A right-hand guard pattern *(8)* and quiet zone *(9)* complete the symbol.

Strategies That Keep the Message Clear

In order to read bar codes accurately, scanners must be able to cope with a large degree of variability in the appearance of symbols. Although all UPC symbols fall within certain structural guidelines, they vary in size, color, and print quality, depending on the kind of package on which they are printed. Sophisticated decoding algorithms ensure that these discrepancies do not throw off the computer's interpretation of the bar code's message.

Variations in symbol size are permissible because scanners measure the relative differences between a symbol's bars and spaces, rather than comparing them, say, to an absolute scale of dimensions. Thus one bar code may have individual modules twice as wide as another, but the scanner will decode both correctly, adjusting its reading in accord with the standard module width established for each separate symbol *(box,*

A decimal one from the bar code's left half is represented by the pattern of bars and spaces shown at left, which translate into a seven-bit binary code. This and all other digits in the left half begin with a space, end with a bar, and contain an odd number of dark modules, or binary ones.

The bar-code pattern for a decimal one the right half conforms to an entirely differ set of rules: It begins with a bar, ends w a space, and contains an even number dark modules *(right).* The two patterns are, fact, exact opposites, with ones in the ri half where there were zeros in the left, a zeros where there were on *page 96).* Even different colors will not alter the reading, so long as bars reflect less of the beam than do spaces; otherwise, the scanner might see zeros for ones and vice versa.

A clever encoding, rather than decoding, technique averts another possible source of confusion. To maintain the brisk pace that justifies the expense of such high-tech systems, check-out clerks must be free to sweep packages across scanners in virtually any orientation—without wasting time lining up bar codes in one particular direction. But the computer must still be able to distinguish a symbol's left half, which identifies the manufacturer, from its right, which identifies the item. As the illustration below and the table at right indicate, it can do so because the numbers in each half are encoded in quite different ways; as a result, a bar code's pattern makes sense even when scanned upside down.

The table below lists the binary codes and bar-code patterns for all ten decimal digits; each digit is represented two different ways, depending on whether it falls in the left or right half of the bar-code symbol. Since bar codes may be scanned in either direction, these differences enable the computer to sort out which side is which so it can interpret the symbol properly.

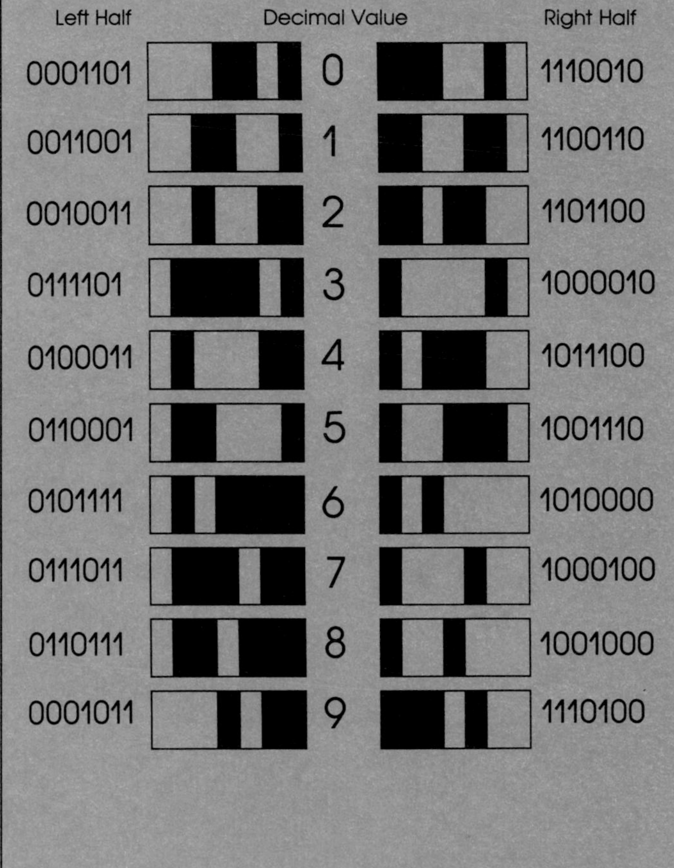

Left Half	Decimal Value	Right Half
0001101	0	1110010
0011001	1	1100110
0010011	2	1101100
0111101	3	1000010
0100011	4	1011100
0110001	5	1001110
0101111	6	1010000
0111011	7	1000100
0110111	8	1001000
0001011	9	1110100

Turning Bars and Bits into Dollars and Cents

A scanning beam *(arrow)* sweeps across the bar-code pattern for a left-half five, which reflects the light back to a detector in the scanner. The detector converts the fluctuating reflections into a continuous, or analog, electrical signal *(below, right)*, with peaks representing the stronger reflections from spaces, and troughs the weak ones from bars.

0 1 1 0 0 0 1

Circuitry within the scanning system converts the analog wave into the discrete, on-off pulses of a digital signal *(below, right)*, which the computer will comprehend as a string of binary digits. A decoding algorithm determines how many identical bits occur in succession in wider spaces and bars by timing how long pulses remain unchanged and comparing this measure to the duration of a single-bit pulse.

0 11 000 1

0 11 0

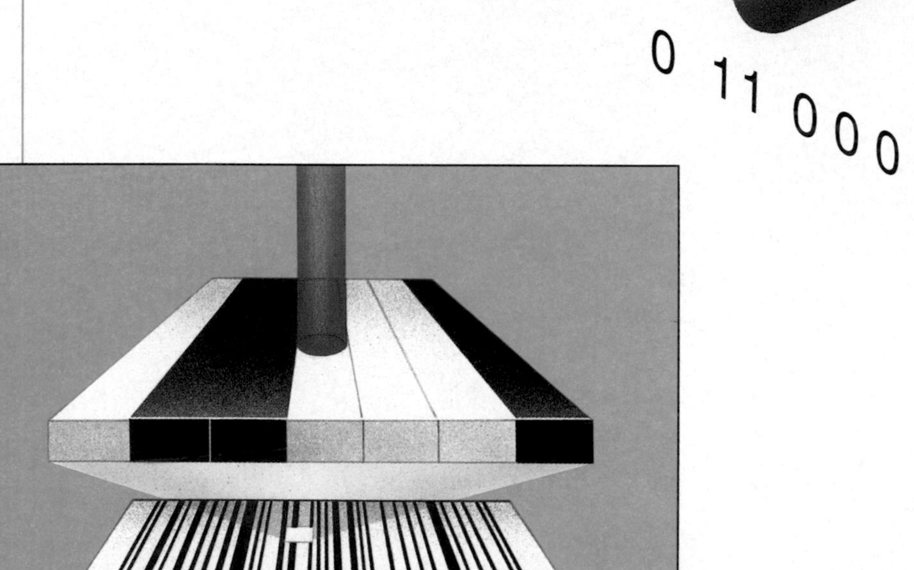

Taking the Measure of a Module

Because different symbols can vary in size, part of the scanner's job is to determine the narrowest bar or space, which always represents a single module, and then apply that dimension as a standard for measuring wider bars and spaces. Using timing logic, a decoding algorithm thus discovers that the second space in the pattern above is three modules wide.

Before a store computer can process the information in a bar code, a whole sequence of transformations must take place. As detailed below, the bar-code stripes printed on a package become first a pattern of reflections, then an electrical analog wave, and finally a digitized signal; only then can the computer go to work interpreting the symbol's data.

All of these changes are set in motion by the scanning apparatus located at the check-out counter. The scanner's prime chore, of course, is directing a beam of light in such a way that its reflections off the bar code can be detected and measured *(pages 104-107)*. But the scanning system also incorporates electronic components and circuitry for translating the varying intensities of light bounced back off bars and spaces into the strings of binary zeros and ones that fuel the computer's processing engine.

Of key importance in the transformation is a decoding algorithm, which determines precisely how many bits each bar and each space comprises. The algorithm must adjust for variations in symbol size from package to package: Working in conjunction with a clock, the algorithm times the on-and-off pulses of the digital signal, then calculates their relative differences to arrive at an exact count of zeros and ones *(box, below left)*.

Equipped with a fully decoded digital message, the computer can now go about identifying which product the code represents and registering the sale *(below)*. In addition, it may invoke file-management programs that keep the store's records updated on an item-by-item basis. The most sophisticated systems even include direct computer links with warehouses so that supplies are restocked virtually automatically.

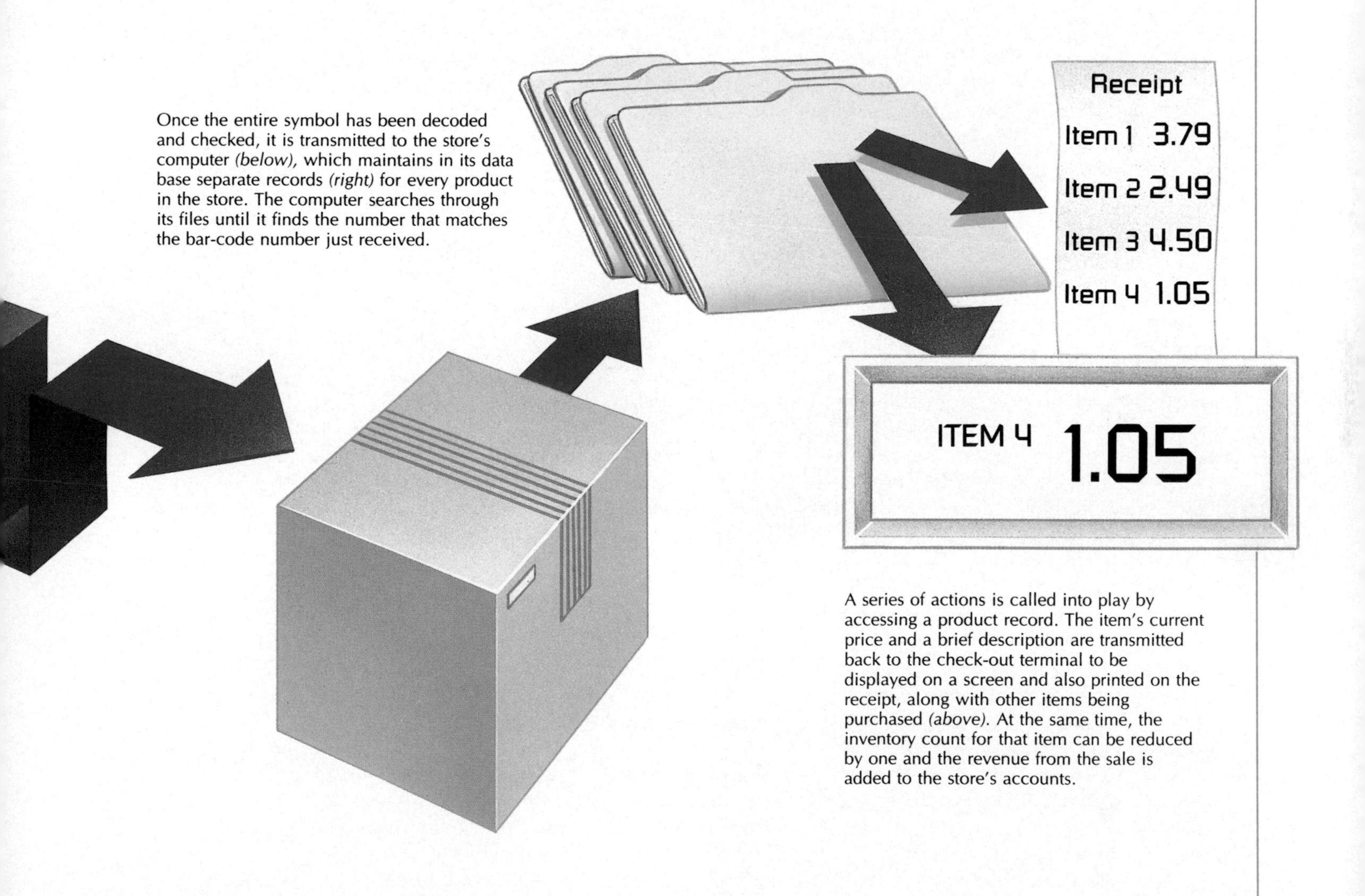

Once the entire symbol has been decoded and checked, it is transmitted to the store's computer *(below)*, which maintains in its data base separate records *(right)* for every product in the store. The computer searches through its files until it finds the number that matches the bar-code number just received.

A series of actions is called into play by accessing a product record. The item's current price and a brief description are transmitted back to the check-out terminal to be displayed on a screen and also printed on the receipt, along with other items being purchased *(above)*. At the same time, the inventory count for that item can be reduced by one and the revenue from the sale is added to the store's accounts.

of twenty-five stitches in a number of sizes, each perfectly and unvaryingly executed, the machine was indeed remarkable. There was, however, a problem: Getting the machine ready to sew had become an obstacle to sewing with it. Dials and levers offered more than 5,000 stitch settings. With so many possibilities, it was difficult to make the machine produce the pattern desired. To match an earlier stitch setting required much trial and error to re-create the dimensions of the original. Furthermore, a stitch more often than not began in the middle of the stitch cycle rather than at the beginning. Turning the machine by hand to arrive at the start of the stitch—a nuisance in itself—often caused the thread to slip from the eye of the needle, making it necessary to rethread the machine.

In August 1971, as a result of Rydz's experiences, a group of Singer engineers was formed to investigate ways of simplifying sewing-machine operation. Eight or so in number, the group came initially under the supervision of Jack Wurst, an engineer with a broad background in electrical devices. Among the group's members was an engineer who specialized in electronic controls, a computer applications expert whose expertise had been to simulate designs for new sewing machines on an IBM mainframe computer, and as Wurst recalled, "an all-round, do-it-yourself dabbler in electronics."

No avenue of investigation—mechanical solutions, electronic ones, or a combination of the two—was barred to Wurst's group. They would examine one approach for a few weeks, write a report on the results, and "slip it under the door," as Wurst later described the process of passing the group's findings to Kircher and Rydz. A week or so later, a refinement or even a new avenue would be suggested, leading to another report. By the first of November, less than three months after the group first met, Kircher and Rydz had decided to turn the sewing machine into an electronically controlled appliance. "I don't think we expected to have arrived at a management decision by that time," recalled Wurst, "but that's the way it worked out. The nice thing was that we were relieved of virtually every other duty for that period."

The engineering group, by now well on the way to becoming a full-fledged development department, determined that the full motion of the teeth that fed the cloth through the machine should be divided into thirty increments and that the needle's full side-by-side motion—called the bight—should be divided into twenty-five increments. That the four-bit word of a microprocessor such as the Intel 4004 offered only sixteen unique combinations of ones and zeros was no obstacle; by linking two words for each feed or bight movement, Singer could have had thirty-two combinations, more than enough. Yet the sewing-machine engineers concentrated on hardwired solutions, just as calculator designers had done in the days before Busicom met Intel. The main reason was cost. The general-purpose Intel 4004 sold for about twice the price of the special-purpose circuits proposed by Singer.

To make the sewing machine sew, stitch instructions were divided into ten-bit chunks of information, five to direct the feed and five to position the needle. A complete pattern might require twenty to thirty such chunks. Each set of stitch instructions was hardwired onto an integrated-circuit chip. To execute a stitch, the five bits representing the feed motion for the first instruction were changed by a digital-to-analog converter to a voltage having a value that depended on the sequence of ones and zeros passed to the converter. This voltage, which corresponded to one of the thirty cloth-feed positions, was routed through an amplifier and other circuitry to a servomotor, which was stimulated by the voltage coming from the amplifier to move the teeth the appropriate distance. With the cloth in the correct position, the five bits controlling the bight raced a second motor that moved the needle to one side or the other, as required by the stitch. This process was repeated for each of the instructions that constituted a stitch. By August 1972, Wurst's team had constructed several working prototypes. Upon seeing them in operation, Singer's president Don Kircher said, "That's exactly what I want."

Three years later, the first electronically controlled sewing machine appeared in stores. It was named the Athena 2000. Like its top-of-the-line predecessor, it offered twenty-five stitches—an ordinary straight stitch and four groups of six construction and decorative stitches. Selecting a stitch became simplicity itself. Instead of manipulating mechanical controls to one of several thousand positions, rotating a four-position electric switch designated one of the four stitch groups, then pressing one of six buttons specified a stitch within the group. A knob governed the size of the pattern. Each time a new stitch was selected, the sewing machine automatically began at the start of the cycle, eliminating the need to turn the machine by hand and to rethread it afterwards. Restoring the machine to a previous setting became foolproof. Sewing-machine construction was simplified as well; the electronic parts occupied less space and were much simpler to build than the precision cams of purely mechanical models.

So successful commercially was the Athena 2000 that nine months passed before Singer caught up with the initial flush of orders. Subsequent versions of the electronic sewing machine incorporated an ever-increasing number of stitches until, in the late 1970s, it became clear that the burden of hardwiring each stitch into the machine was fast becoming unbearable, just as had the one-function-one-circuit approach to building electronic calculators. By this time, microprocessors capable of handling eight-bit words, or bytes, were available and inexpensive enough to be built into a sewing machine. In 1979, Singer settled on a microprocessor produced by the Rockwell International Corporation, one of many companies that began to produce such chips during the 1970s. In 1981, the Model 2010 became available in stores.

A MICROPROCESSOR INVASION

The sewing machine is archetypical of the computerization of appliances. As the quantities of microprocessors produced each year increased from several hundred in 1972 to millions by the 1980s, their price steadily declined. Consequently the microprocessor could be found almost anywhere, alerting a midnight refrigerator raider that the door has been left ajar, regulating the emissions from a magnetron tube in a microwave oven as it thaws a roast for dinner, adjusting the mixture of gasoline and air fed to an automobile engine, or controlling the lens aperture and shutter speed of a camera.

Even children's toys were affected. A microprocessor embedded in the torso of a doll named Julie controlled a speech-synthesis chip manufactured by Texas Instruments that enabled the doll to recognize the sound of her owner's voice and respond to more than a hundred key words, including her own name and the phrase "be quiet." To endow Julie with additional vocabulary, her owner could plug in a credit-card-size memory module that contained more than 64,000 bytes of electronic personality. Outfitted with motion detectors, Julie would inquire "Where are we going?" when she was picked up. Photodetectors in the doll's eyes prompted her to ask for dark glasses whenever she was carried into the sunshine. A thermal sensor connected to the microprocessor made it possible for Julie to request a sweater when the temperature fell ten degrees or more—as might occur when the doll was taken outdoors—or to complain of being too warm when the temperature rose.

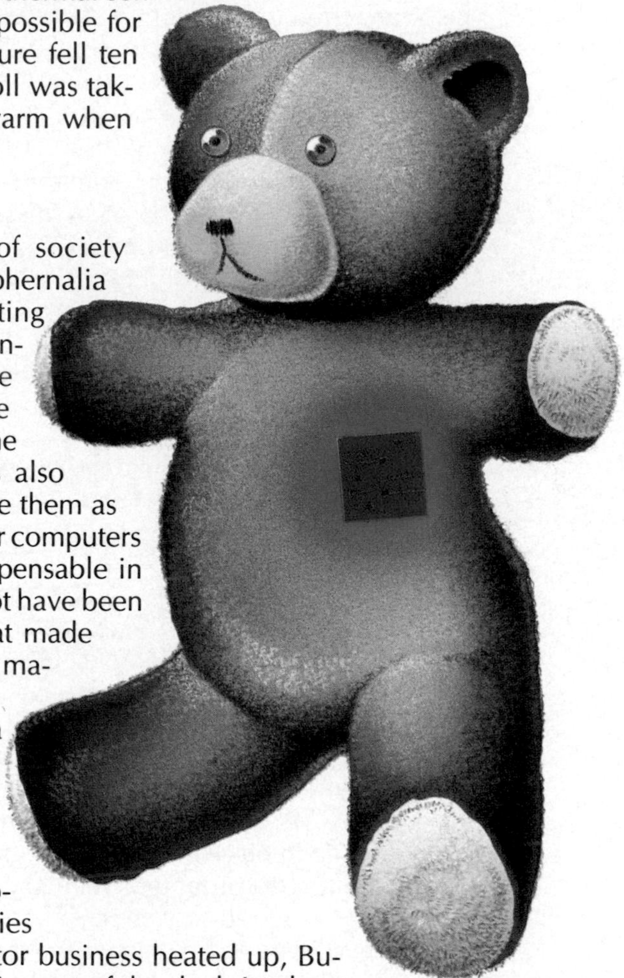

A GREATER SIGNIFICANCE

Though far-reaching, the computerization of society through its appliances, toys, and other paraphernalia was superficial compared with the penetrating changes already wrought in the world by mainframe computers and their increasingly capable operating systems. Yet simultaneously with the broadcast seeding of microprocessors across the surface of society, these computers on chips also began to evolve in a direction that would make them as capable, in many respects, as the huge multiuser computers that had already come to be considered indispensable in many industries. These developments would not have been possible were it not for the same advance that made practical the computerization of the sewing machine—the eight-bit microprocessor.

This giant step forward had come about as a direct result of the enthusiastic acceptance of Intel's 4004 chip by electronics hobbyists eager to have a computer of their own, regardless of how rudimentary it might be. When Intel first began manufacturing the chip, every one produced went to Busicom, as the two companies had agreed. When competition in the calculator business heated up, Busicom negotiated a lower price for the 4004. As part of the deal, Intel got the right to sell the chip to whomever wished to buy it.

The lower price was little help to Busicom. In the end, the company could not compete in the calculator market with firms that produced their own microprocessors, and Busicom eventually went out of business. For Intel, however, the right to market the 4004 independently would prove to be a gold mine. Some within Intel doubted that many would buy the chip, and they wondered what the few who purchased it could possibly use it for. Nevertheless, in November of 1971, an Intel advertisement for the chip appeared in electronics trade journals. "Announcing a new era of integrated electronics," touted the copywriter. "A microprogrammable computer on a chip!" By the following

February, Intel had already sold to electronics tinkerers $85,000 worth of the 4004 chips at $200 each.

At about the time that Intel began marketing the 4004, a company called Computer Technology Corporation (which later became Datapoint) approached Intel with a request for a more capable microprocessor. CTC wanted to build an intelligent terminal for mainframe computers—one with computing capabilities of its own—to replace the dumb terminals that were then commonly attached to the machines.

The four-bit chip was unsuitable mostly because the alphabet outnumbered its sixteen unique combinations of ones and zeros. At least thirty-six such combinations are necessary to accommodate all twenty-six letters and ten numerals. Additional such combinations are required if there are to be both capital and lowercase letters, punctuation marks, and mathematical symbols. Intel felt that an eight-bit processor, offering 256 arrangements of ones and zeros, would more than suffice. The result, in 1972, was the 8008.

CTC never used the chip, but Intel sold it on the open market. At $120 apiece, the 8008 offered greater potential for less money than the 4004. One of the first to buy an 8008 was an electronics tinkerer named Jonathan Titus, who in the autumn of 1973 used the chip to build a computer he called the Mark-8. The works fit into a plain metal box with twenty-four lights on the front—one for each of the eight bits in a byte of data or program code, plus sixteen others to report on the internal status of the machine. The lights were accompanied by a number of controls, including eight on-off switches that corresponded to the bits in a data or program byte and a button for entering information into the computer's small memory. The Mark-8 appeared on the front cover of the July 1974 issue of *Radio-Electronics,* which featured the headline "Build the Mark-8, Your Personal Minicomputer." The cost of the components for a Mark-8—including an 8008 microprocessor; additional, prewired circuit boards; and the metal box—was about $250. Some twenty-five hundred people actually built the device.

For the money and the time necessary to assemble the device, a builder of the Mark-8 got precious little in the way of utility. Instructions and data for the machine were entered one byte at a time by flipping the switches to represent each bit—off for a zero, on for a one—then pressing the button to send the byte to the computer's memory. For example, to make the Mark-8 add two and three required five settings of the switches just to instruct the machine to add two figures and display the answer. Another switch setting to represent the two and yet another for the three made a total of seven. The result would appear as ones, represented by glowing lights on the face of the machine, and zeros, indicated by unlit lights. If no errors occurred in setting the switches, the lights would show 00110101, which stands for five in the widely used computer code ASCII. As troublesome as this procedure may seem, it was much the same situation that faced the first programmers of early mainframe computers like ENIAC and the IBM 701.

And the same was true of the next computer based on a microprocessor, the Altair 8800. This machine was designed in 1974 by Edward Roberts, a businessman looking for a new product to rescue his foundering calculator-kit company, Micro Instrumentation and Telemetry Systems (MITS). Introduced as a kit in the January 1975 issue of *Popular Electronics,* the Altair had as its brain a redesigned 8008 chip from Intel called the 8080. Among other improvements, this new IC executed instructions much faster than its predecessor did. In the end, however, the Altair could not save MITS. In 1979 the company went out of business.

By 1976, Intel was no longer the sole producer of eight-bit microprocessors. Zilog, a new company founded by a former Intel engineer, produced the Z-80. Motorola introduced a chip called the 6800. A company named MOS Technology developed the 6502 microprocessor. Each of these chips became the nerve center for a family of computers that were built, in many cases, by several companies.

A SYSTEM FOR MICROS

But if this new kind of computer was to become anything more than a curiosity, the machines had to become much more utilitarian—and a lot easier to use. The missing ingredient was an operating system, a set of programs that would do for the microprocessor-powered computer what GM/IO, SOS, and OS/360 had accomplished for mainframe computers: control peripheral devices like displays, printers, and data-storage units; allow users to move, copy, and otherwise manipulate files of data; tell the computer when to start an application program and when to stop it; and a host of other routines necessary for the moment-to-moment operation of the computer.

Manufacturers of microprocessors left the writing of operating systems to the computer makers, with the result that the availability and quality of this crucial software varied widely from company to company; MITS, for example, never produced an operating system for the Altair. Because every company's computer had a different repertoire of these basic programs, applications software had to be substantially rewritten for each brand of machine. One software developer, Michael Shrayer, wrote nearly eighty versions of his ground-breaking program Electric Pencil, the first word-processing software for microcomputers, as this new breed of computer was called. However, most programmers were not so accommodating as Shrayer, preferring to write software for just a few of the most popular computers and thus severely limiting the choice of programs available to purchasers of other brands.

Making software compatible with the wide variety of hardware on the market demanded a common operating system, one that would work with a variety of eight-bit computers. Gary Kildall, a professor of computer science at the University of California in Berkeley, came up with one.

Kildall had been an early purchaser of the Intel 4004 microprocessor. In the course of programming it to perform navigational computations, Kildall became intrigued by the chip's inner workings, so much so that he persuaded Intel to hire him as a consultant, that is, as an independent contractor for tasks that fell outside the expertise of the company's integrated-circuit engineering staff.

Kildall's first project for Intel was to write a programming language for the 8080 called PL/M, a scaled-down version of a mainframe language known as PL/I, which was widely used for scientific, business, and computer-systems programming. In order to make PL/M as much like PL/I as possible—thereby minimizing the amount of time required to create the new language—Kildall needed an operating system capable of performing many of the same tasks in much the same way that a mainframe operating system that used PL/I accomplished them. In particular, Kildall's new language required an operating system that permitted data and programs to be stored on magnetic disks.

Though Kildall was a masterful programmer, he knew too little of disk technology to make the devices function with his operating system. So, in late 1973, he enlisted John Torode, an expert in such matters and a colleague at Berkeley whom Kildall had known since graduate-school days at the University of Washington. Within a few weeks, the pair had for the 8080 a working operating system that Kildall christened CP/M. Initially, the letters stood for Control Program/Monitor; later they came to mean Control Program for Microprocessors.

CP/M was a boon for owners of computers based on the 8080 chip, whether or not they planned to write programs in PL/M. Not only would the operating system work with most computers based on the 8080 (some computers had insufficient memory for CP/M or were designed with idiosyncracies that prevented the use of the operating system), it was also compatible with a variety of computers built around other microprocessors similar to the 8080, including Zilog's Z-80 chip. Any software written to work with CP/M would also run on those machines.

For the time being, other kinds of microcomputers were out of luck. CP/M simply would not work with eight-bit microprocessors that were not clones or improvements of the 8080, unless the operating system was partially rewritten to accommodate the differences between the two chips. In a master stroke, Kildall—Torode had already gone in pursuit of other interests—reorganized the operating system, collecting into a single section those parts of the program that had to be rewritten before CP/M would work with microprocessors unrelated to the 8080. As a result, it became a simple task to adapt CP/M to a wide range of computers.

The broad compatibility between CP/M and microcomputers that Kildall's revision made possible permitted programmers to write a single version of software that would run on many machines. A flood of programs began to appear: spreadsheet software for business, word-processing software for writers of every stripe, educational software, and new computer languages. With CP/M began the spread of desktop computers, one to an individual, computerizing the world outside the air-conditioned realms of the mainframes.

A DOUBLE-EDGED SWORD

In some ways, CP/M retarded the spread of microcomputers even as it accelerated the process. As is typical of any operating system, for example, CP/M required that each data file have a name before it could be stored on a disk. However, a name could be no more than eleven characters in length. A frequent user of a CP/M computer could soon generate a long list of cryptic file names that might reveal next to nothing about each file's contents. Operating-system commands, the merely convenient as well as the truly essential, were unmemorable at best. For example, to transfer a file named "business" from one floppy-disk drive to another, a common operation if only to make a spare copy of important data, the computer operator had to type: PIP B:=A:BUSINESS, in

Reading Bar Codes with Beams of Light

The optical scanning devices that read a bar code's digital message come in a variety of designs, as shown here and on the next three pages. But they all follow the same basic principle: They illuminate a symbol with a narrow beam of light that traverses the pattern, then gather the varying reflections from dark bars and light spaces and translate them into binary code. Although arrangements differ, certain key components are also common to all: a light source to generate the beam, mirrors and lenses to direct it toward the symbol, and a light-sensitive detector that both registers reflections and converts them to electrical signals *(pages 96-97)*.

The two major classes of scanners are fixed-beam and moving-beam devices. Fixed-beam scanners are often employed in factory settings; the stationary ray these scanners project reads codes as items move by, for example, on an assembly line. But many hand-held scanners, such as the light pen below, also use fixed beams, relying on hand motion to trace the beam across the symbol's width. Light pens must touch the symbol to obtain accurate readings, and their decoding circuitry must include complex algorithms to deal with the inconsistent speeds at which the beam may be moved across symbols.

Moving-beam scanners, on the other hand, sweep a beam across a fixed path at rates of forty scans per second or more. Moving parts within the device, such as the oscillating mirror in the laser scanner at right, guarantee a predictable reading speed that makes decoding more precise. These devices also work a foot or so away from a symbol; all the operator need do is aim and fire.

A light pen projects a fixed beam and must be manually drawn across a bar-code symbol to read it. Typically, a light-emitting diode (LED) in the pen generates a broad beam of light, which bounces off a mirror pitched at a forty-five-degree angle and is focused through a lens into the small spot that strikes the symbol. The beam reflects off the symbol back into the pen, is refocused by the lens, and then passes through an aperture in the mirror to be sensed and converted to an electrical signal by the photodetector.

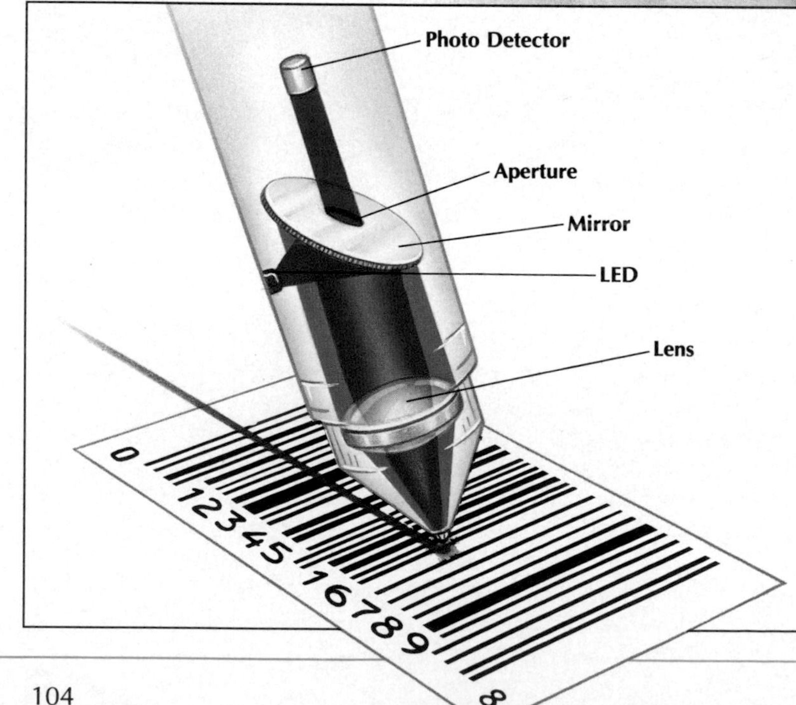

This hand-held laser scanner has internal mechanisms that automatically move its beam of light across the symbol. The helium-neon laser—activated by the trigger—produces a beam of light, which is refracted by a prism through the lens to the oscillating mirror. The mirror shakes back and forth very rapidly, sweeping the beam in a wide enough field to cover the bar code. The more diffuse reflected light passes back through the scanner's window to the mirror and is redirected to the lens, to be focused into a narrower beam for the photodetector.

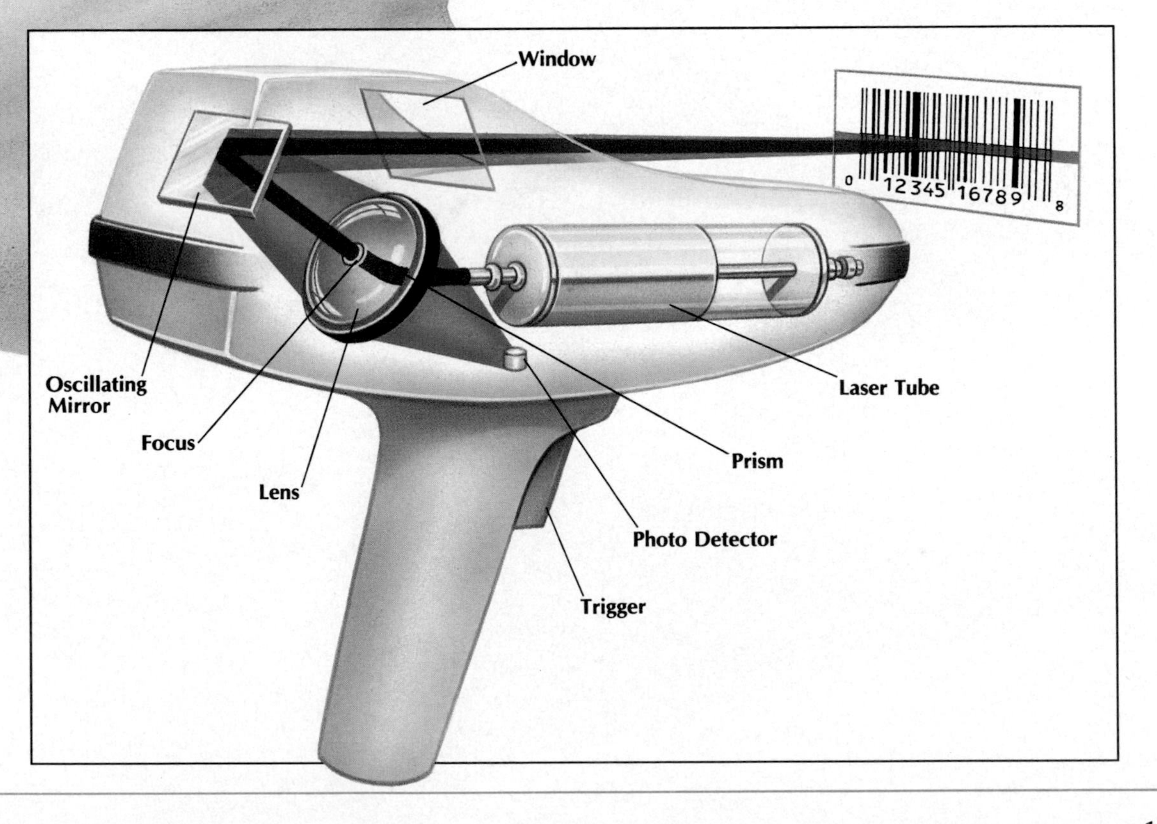

A Scanner That Spins a Web of Light

Grocery-store scanners represent the ultimate in bar-code-reading technology. Designed to handle a high-volume flow of items as quickly as possible, these built-in devices cast an intricate pattern of light—produced by one beam rapidly reflected off many mirrors—onto packages held above them, eliminating the need for any time-consuming alignment or orientation of the bar-code symbol; the pattern's fine weave is almost sure to pick up the code on the item's very first pass over the scanner.

Generating such a pattern requires a fairly complex set of

Although the scanner below appears to the eye to project a grid of laser light onto the can at right, the pattern is actually traced by a single beam moving so rapidly as to create the illusion of multiple crisscrossing and parallel lines. By covering each item with a weave of light, the scanner virtually guarantees that one of its beam's paths will successfully cross the entire bar code—no matter how the item is oriented.

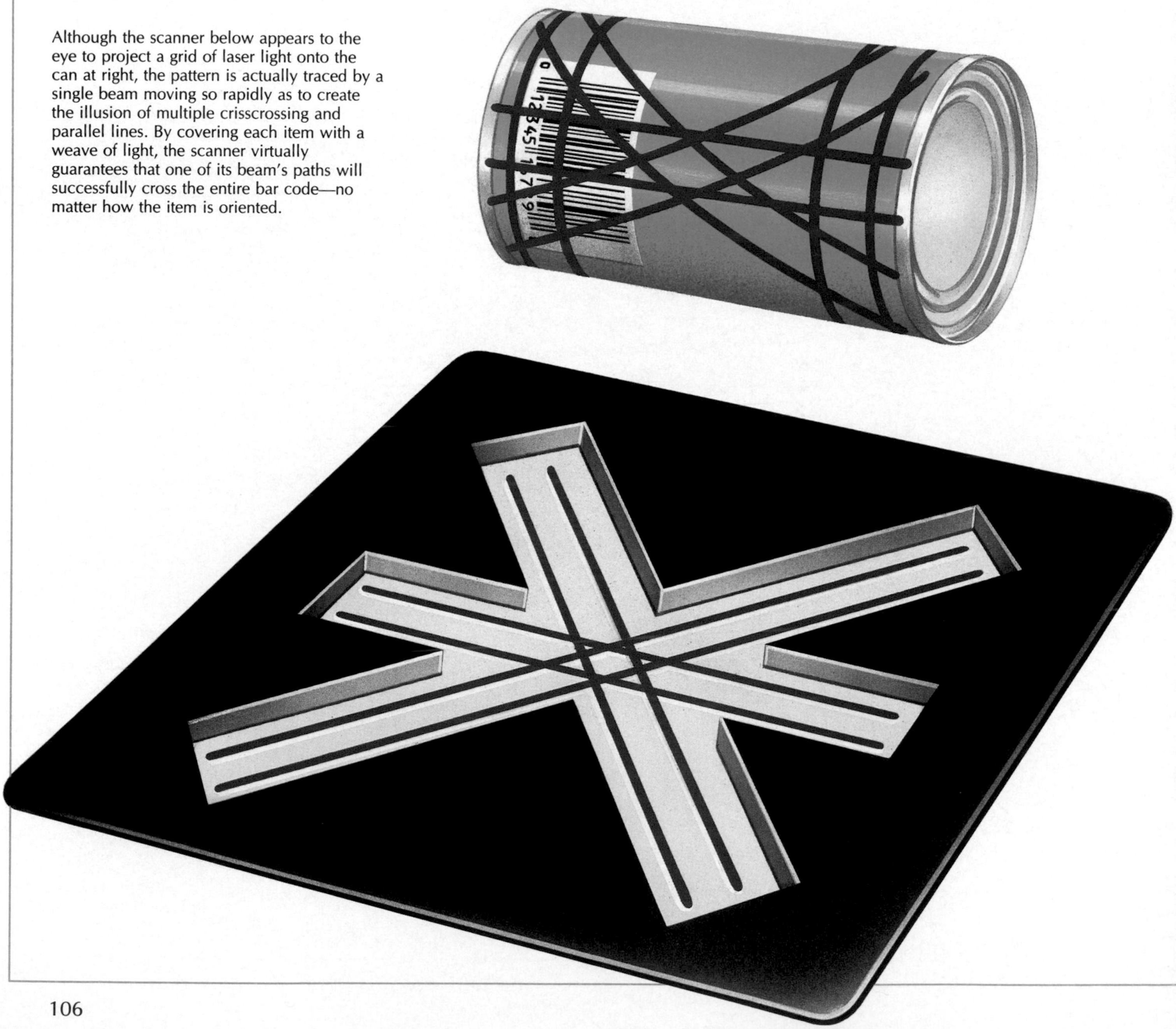

optical components, but the entire unit can easily be incorporated into the typical check-out counter; the box measures some twenty inches long, less than a foot wide, and just over ten inches deep. Window shapes vary with different models; the intersecting strips of the one below allow just enough room for the beam to trace its design while protecting the glass as much as possible from being bumped by cans or bottles.

Like the hand-held device on page 105, this scanner relies on one moving part to make the beam sweep: A mirror wheel, spinning counterclockwise at a rate of 6,000 revolutions per minute, continuously alters the light's path. But the real secret to achieving such a mesh of light is the series of pattern-generating mirrors off which the beam bounces *(below);* positioned at precise angles, the beams direct the laser light along routes carefully calculated by system designers to offer the maximum coverage of the items being scanned. And on the return trip from the bar code, these same mirrors help guide the reflected beam toward the scanner's photodetector, where the all-important work of translating the different reflections begins.

A complex array of components guides the scanner's beam into the pattern outlined at far left. From the laser tube, the beam is directed by two small routing mirrors to the first of three larger mirrors, then through a lens to a rotating mirror wheel. The wheel sweeps the beam across the two pattern-generating mirrors, which direct the beam through the window's strips. The reflected beam hits the bar code and then returns by the same path but is redirected by the lens and mirror toward the detector.

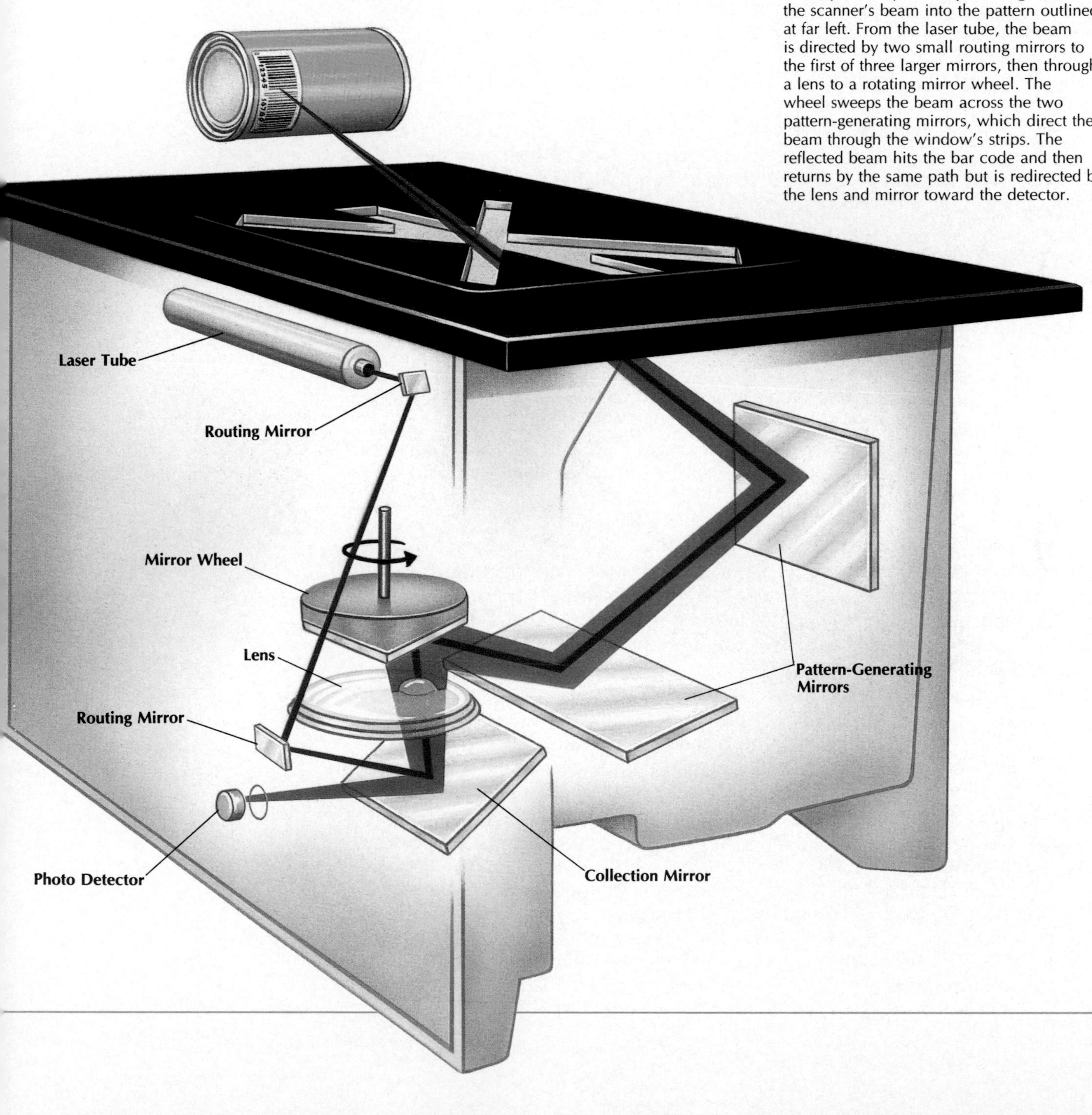

which PIP stood for Peripheral Interchange Program, the portion of CP/M that accomplished the transfer; B: referred to the disk drive making the copy; and A: represented the drive containing the disk with the original. Moreover, if a keystroke were missed or an incorrect key depressed while typing a command, the entire sequence of characters had to be retyped, a tedious procedure when CP/M commands could exceed thirty keystrokes.

Despite its shortcomings, CP/M was the leading operating system for microcomputers until IBM introduced its Personal Computer in August of 1981. IBM's reputation for reliability and service provided its microcomputer an entrée to the business world not available to machines of suspiciously home-brew origins, such as those made at the time by Tandy/Radio Shack and Apple Computer, each of which supplied an operating system for its own machines.

IBM initially approached Kildall about licensing CP/M to run on its new computer. When negotiations failed, IBM turned to Microsoft, a computer software company belonging to a youthful software genius named Bill Gates. He had written a microcomputer version of the programming language BASIC that IBM had already arranged to supply with their computers, but at the time, Microsoft had no operating system to offer. So Gates purchased one from a small company called Seattle Computer Products, renamed it MS-DOS (Microsoft Disk Operating System), and licensed it to IBM.

So alike were MS-DOS and CP/M that some commands were common to both, though CP/M's more odious ones had been made less so. For example, the name of the program to duplicate a file was changed to "copy," and the syntax was altered to make the command easier to remember—COPY BUSINESS B:. In addition, MS-DOS made it possible to change an incorrectly entered command without retyping it from the beginning. Within a few years, the IBM PC became the best-selling microcomputer on the market, and MS-DOS soon eclipsed CP/M.

A MATTER OF USER FRIENDLINESS

Initially, operating systems for computers such as the IBM PC and for others produced by Apple and Tandy allowed a single individual to do one task at a time with the device, a reflection of the one man, one machine philosophy that made the computers so seductive. Before long, however, new operating-system capabilities began to appear. Other operating systems were written that, with the installation of additional circuitry in a personal computer, allowed it to serve as a central repository for data and programs accessible to other such computers wired together in a network. As early as 1979, for example, Kildall wrote an advanced version of CP/M, called MP/M, that embodied some of these features.

To make the computer easier to use—and perhaps more attractive to people who had so far passed it by—operating systems evolved in which the person sitting at the computer no longer had to remember and type an obscure sequence of words, letters, and symbols to coax something out of the machine, but merely had to select a command by pointing at one in a list of options that appeared on the computer screen. In one system, a fingertip activated a touch-sensitive screen. In others, a pointer that appears on the monitor is moved among command menus by rolling an electronic device called a mouse across the surface of a desk or a table. Pressing a button on the mouse spurs the machine to action.

THE TRANSFORMATION OF A MACHINE

Each advance in this direction spread the microcomputer a little more widely across society. The simplification of CP/M commands in their reincarnation as MS-DOS, the invention of push-button operating systems for personal computers, and the foolproofing of word-processing and accounting software, for example, that allow personal computers to pay their way—all are part of the general-purpose computer's evolution from a monster that only a technician could love toward an electronic servant that approaches a sewing machine or a microwave oven in its ease of operation.

Indeed, when a microprocessor-based computer is assigned a narrow range of tasks analogous, say, to the variety of stitches offered by a sewing machine or the numerous combinations of cooking times and power settings that permit a microwave oven to quickly take the refrigerator chill off leftover chicken or to cook a complete meal, there is little to distinguish the computer from such an appliance.

A SMART BRICK

An example of a computer masquerading as an appliance is the one that is used by couriers of Federal Express, the original overnight-delivery-guaranteed air-express company and a success story rarely equaled in the annals of American business. Called the SuperTracker, the computer is a hand-held device less than the length of a brick and about half as wide. The SuperTracker's purpose is to permit Federal Express to track a package from the minute one courier picks it up from a customer until another courier delivers it to the addressee. This ability to get a fix on the package itself—and not a piece-of-paper stand-in for the package—gives the company the confidence to promise its customers that they can learn where a package is within half an hour of telephoning a Federal Express agent.

The SuperTracker was developed to Federal Express specifications by Handheld Products, Inc., a small North Carolina firm that specializes in making "customized products that fit into an existing environment," said David Dietzel, SuperTracker project manager. The six-person company had developed a memory-expansion attachment for a Hewlett-Packard calculator and, for a Texas Instruments machine, a module that calculated income taxes. In less than four months, Handheld Products produced a device that worked. "It was ugly," recalled Dietzel, but it demonstrated all the capabilities that Federal Express needed—a small display and keyboard, and the ability to decode the type of bar code that Federal Express used for airbill numbers.

The SuperTracker contained an eight-bit microprocessor that was originally designed, as it happens, to control microwave ovens. In that role, the chip required only rudimentary control instructions, but in the SuperTracker, its functions are managed by a multifeatured operating system that, in almost every respect, is the equivalent of the operating systems found at work in most personal computers.

Written by Handheld Products's programmers and later extensively expanded by Federal Express, the operating system handles a wide variety of peripheral devices, such as a keyboard, a small screen to display messages and prompts for the courier, a bar-code scanner *(pages 104-105)*, and an optical communications device, as well as a built-in modem for telephone transmission of package information in the event that the optical system fails.

Where a desktop-computer operating system stores data and programs on disks, the SuperTracker operating system stores such information in memory. If data or a program in one part of the memory is somehow rendered inoperative—for example, by a pulse of static electricity, a hazard for any computer—new information or software is copied from another area of memory. Should all the computer's memory be affected, a simpler but no less complete version of the software resides permanently in read-only memory, which is unperturbed by static electric discharges or even loss of power from the computer's internal batteries. The operating system is also capable of multitasking. That is, it can perform several operating-system functions simultaneously, such as watching for input from the keyboard at the same time that the computer functions as a bar-code scanner.

These features, mated with software that leads a courier step by step through the package pickup and delivery procedures, make learning how to operate the computer exceptionally easy. A courier who is already familiar with the vocabulary of Federal Express operations, says Chris Demos, a Federal Express official who has been involved with the project since its earliest stages, can learn to work the SuperTracker in thirty minutes with no instruction other than a short "geography lesson" on the keyboard. In what Demos believes to be "the largest, industrial training project ever," Federal Express has trained more than 20,000 couriers and other personnel in the use of the SuperTracker and related equipment.

Pickup of a package begins with a scan of the bar code printed on the Federal Express airbill, a combination mailing label and receipt with a unique ten-digit number used to track a package from its point of origin to its destination. The SuperTracker signals a successful scan of the bar code with a beep, then displays a series of questions for the courier to answer about the package, including the type of service requested, special-handling codes, and the zip code of the intended recipient.

The SuperTracker's response includes a routing code and the name of the state, derived from the zip code to which the package is being shipped. If the state differs from the one written on the airbill, the courier can correct the mistake at the time that the package is accepted for shipment. The routing code permits sorting of packages so that they can be loaded, nearly without error, onto aircraft appropriate to their destinations.

Returning to the van, the courier slides the SuperTracker into a receptacle of a computer terminal mounted in the cab. Automatically, the SuperTracker begins to transfer information about the package to the terminal by means of the light-emitting diode used to read the bar code. In this mode of operation, however, the light sends out pulses of light that represent package information being passed from memory as ones and zeros. The terminal in the van transmits the information by radio through a communications network to IBM computers at Federal Express headquarters in Memphis, Tennessee. There, the information becomes available to service representatives, for answering customers' questions about their shipments.

Thereafter, each time the package comes to a Federal Express transshipment point—as it is loaded into a cargo container at the local airport, when it arrives at the destination airport, during the process of sending it to the local base of van operations in the addressee's city, as the package is loaded into the van for delivery, and again when the courier hands it over to the addressee—the airbill bar code is scanned by a SuperTracker or a similar computer designed to be carried in a delivery van. Among the advantages derived from tracking a package so closely: The rare mistake in routing can often be discovered before the package reaches the wrong destination, often allowing the company to deliver the item on time despite an error, or at least to notify the customer that the shipment will be delayed.

AUTOMATED MAINTENANCE

At the end of the day, a courier slips his SuperTracker into a receptacle in a wall-mounted unit called a smart base. "It's kind of an eerie deal," said Dietzel. "At clandestine hours—two or three o'clock in the morning—the smart base comes alive, and all these lights start flashing. The SuperTrackers start beeping. It's a total shakedown of the system." The computer's batteries are recharged, its bar-code reader is checked, and its ability to communicate with the terminal in the van is confirmed. The company's airplane schedules, package-routing information, and the software that prompts the courier through pickup and delivery procedures are verified. If any such information or program is incorrect or out of date, it is updated from correct versions maintained in the IBM mainframes in Memphis. At the conclusion of the process, which takes several hours, a light glows green if the SuperTracker has passed the examination. An amber light or a red one sends the courier next morning to the stockroom for a replacement computer.

As remarkable as the Federal Express system is for its high degree of automation and its ease of use, it is perhaps even more noteworthy for the degree of integration that has been achieved between diverse hardware and software. Federal Express officials point out that implementing each of the network's components—the on-line package data base maintained by the company's IBMs, the terminals in the vans, and the multiple thousands of microprocessor-controlled SuperTrackers—presented major challenges. But those paled before the even greater complexities of assuring that three kinds of computers, each with a different operating system and each mutually unintelligible to the others, could be linked together in a reliable, worldwide network.

For Federal Express, committed to offering its customers an unprecedented degree of service and determined to control the finest details of its business, the benefits of computerizing its operations have outweighed the costs. Indeed the very idea behind Federal Express was predicated upon computers. Fred Smith, the company's visionary founder, appreciated even as a student at Yale University in the mid-1960s, at a time when operating systems for mainframes were just evolving from batch processing, that the world would become dependent on computers almost to the point of addiction.

A DIMNESS OF FORESIGHT

Smith's Yale business professor rated as just average his student's idea to charge a premium for fast, reliable delivery of parts necessary to bring ailing computers back on line. And business academia was not alone in this implied misjudgment. Few have predicted accurately the future importance of computers, the extent to which they would pervade society. The pace of the world would slow perceptibly without them. Productivity would decline drastically in endeavors that have become dependent on these electronic wonders. All kinds of activities, from enrolling students in college courses to tracking down tax evaders, would take more time and, more often than not, would produce far less satisfactory results. Some enterprises—Federal Express, for example—would simply disappear.

There is, to be sure, a darker side to the computerization of society. People have been wrongly denied credit, or thrown into jail because of information recorded falsely in vast data bases. Public facts that were once reasonably private by virtue of their inaccessibility are now widely known. Being evicted from an apartment, for example, may qualify a person for entry in a file that owners of rental property sometimes consult before accepting a new tenant. With the computerization of credit cards, social security numbers, and drivers' licenses, individuals are known everywhere. Though some object to the pervasiveness of computers, on balance, the pluses seem to outweigh the minuses. And there is every reason to expect that computers will expand their influence over virtually every aspect of daily life.

A Revolution in Retailing

4

In retail merchandising, the difference between success and failure is often determined by inventory control—achieving a proper balance between having too much stock on hand and having too little. A store that frequently runs out of merchandise throws away sales. But a store that stocks much more than its customers will buy quickly goes broke: suppliers must be paid for the goods, and warehousing costs can be ruinous.

Before the advent of computers, close control of inventory was not economically practical. Stores carry so many items—perhaps 450,000 in a large department store—that manual comparison of sales outflow against suppliers' shipments inflow might take weeks of processing paper records. But now the spreading automation of the entire stream of merchandise, from purchase order to supplier to warehouse to store to check-out counter or point-of-sale terminal, promises to provide daily, hourly, and in some cases even minute-to-minute data on inventory.

As explained on the following pages, a large department-store chain accomplishes this miracle by a system that depends on three elements: bar codes, scanners that read the codes automatically, and a network of computers linking check-out terminals and branch stores to the chain headquarters. Different items carry different bar codes; each bar code leads to a unique product record, stored on disk, that contains a wealth of information about the item, including its supplier, price, and quantity in stock. At various steps in the retail cycle, as an item is received at the warehouse, distributed to the branches, and finally sold, a clerk reads the item's bar code into the computer system with a scanner, and the product file is updated automatically.

In the course of a day, this cycle generates an avalanche of information, which may be useful well beyond the discipline of inventory control. Analyzed by computer, the data can paint an up-to-the-minute picture of trends in the marketplace, reveal the comparative performance of a particular store or even an individual employee, and—perhaps most valuable of all—allow managers to determine strategies that might give the chain a competitive edge.

A Revolution in Retailing

Computer Networks to Track Merchandise

Whether a retail chain consists of three stores or three dozen, its computers function in a hierarchical arrangement like the one illustrated here. At the top of the hierarchy is a "host computer" at headquarters—in this example, administrative offices and a central warehouse. It is linked by special telephone lines to a computer installed at each branch store. Called an in-store processor or controller, this branch-store computer is in turn connected to each of a store's point-of-sale terminals. The connections might be established by a local area network—a combination of computer software and hardware that allows terminals to communicate with the in-store processor.

Every transaction at a terminal—sale, refund, or return of merchandise—is reported to the in-store processor, which records the information and later transmits it to the host computer at headquarters. The host computer, which already holds data on shipments from suppliers, can thus calculate an accurate inventory for each item at all stores as well as prepare a variety of reports on sales activity.

In an expanded system, inventory control and accounting may be almost totally computerized. The host can be programmed to communicate directly to computers of the chain's suppliers, automatically placing orders when stock at the central warehouse drops below a predetermined level.

Some retail organizations are so large that they may find it advantageous to add another level to the computer hierarchy. A nationwide chain of stores, for example, might have several regional headquarters, each supervising a group of branches. The regional headquarters would have its own intermediate host computer, interposed between individual stores and the national headquarters, to collect local data and prepare area reports.

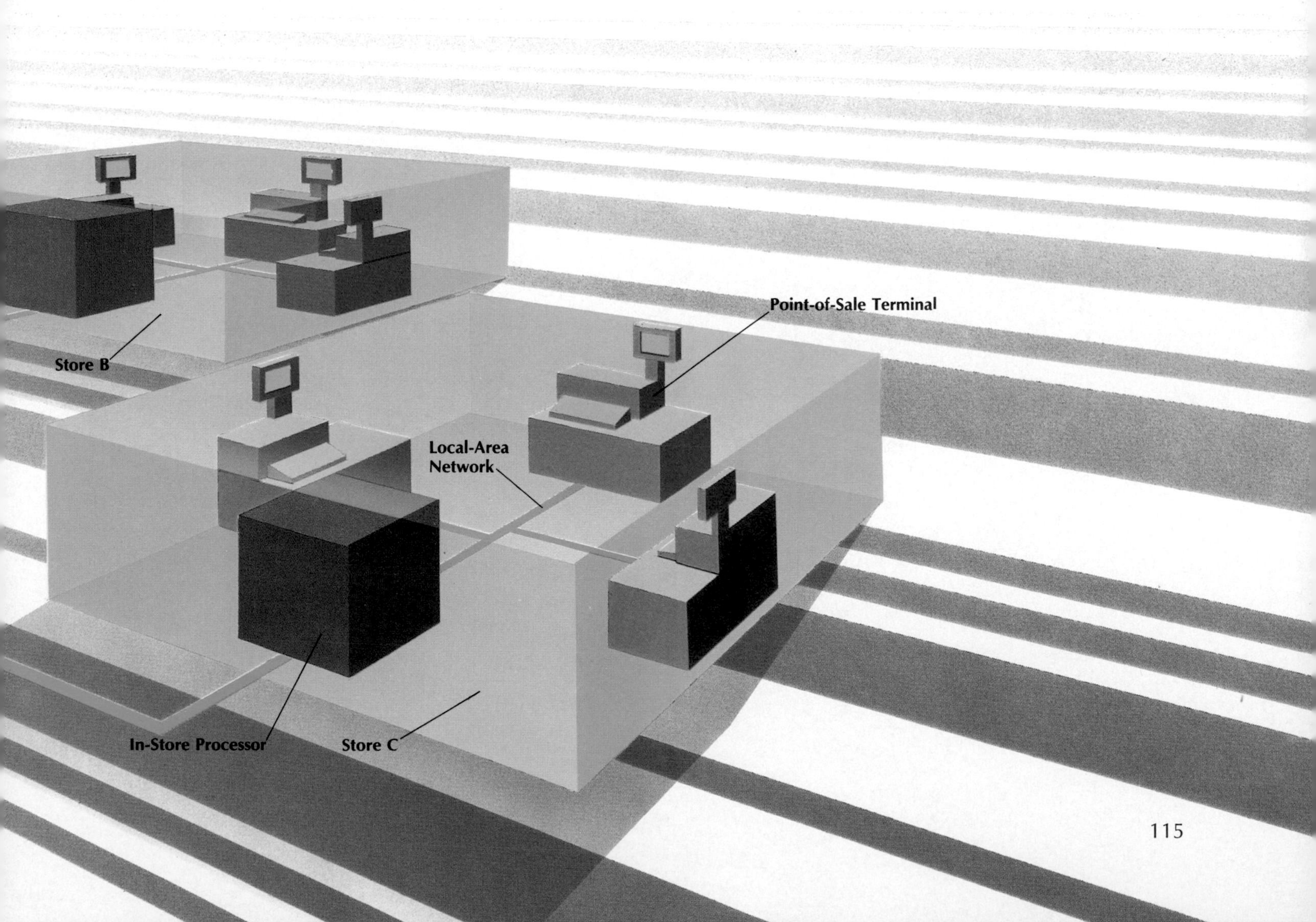

A Revolution in Retailing

At the Warehouse: Checking in the Goods

Stocking a department store chain requires that merchandise be moved from place to place many times—factory to supplier's warehouse to central warehouse to branch store and sales floor. At every transfer point, goods must be counted and then compared to an order. Computers relieve people of much of this tedium, beginning, in advanced systems, with an automatically generated purchase order and thereafter electronically monitoring the flow of merchandise.

This automated tracking is made possible by the use of at least two different bar codes, both generally applied by the supplier. One—the UPC code *(pages 92-94)*—appears on a tag on each item to identify it. The other, generated by scanning each tag as the item is placed in a shipping carton, is placed on the carton to serve as an identification for a packing list of the carton's contents.

When a truck delivers cartons to the central warehouse, a clerk begins the receiving process illustrated below and outlined in the box at the lower right. First, the purchase-order number is entered into a terminal, signaling the chain's host computer to recall from its files the original order plus related data already transmitted by the supplier: shipping information and packing lists for all cartons sent. Next, the clerk uses a laser-gun scanner to read the bar code on each carton as it comes off the truck. The host computer uses the information decoded by the laser-scanner system to log in the merchandise, adding it to inventory, and to compare it to the goods listed on the purchase order. In the event of a discrepancy, an employee is alerted. Finally, the computer automatically records the cost of the goods as a sum the chain owes.

Goods may be transferred immediately to the stores, or, as is frequently the case with staple items, stocked in the warehouse for later distribution. In either case, merchandise is scanned and the computer files are updated each time goods are moved before reaching the sales floor—typically, once as an item leaves the warehouse and again as it arrives at a branch store.

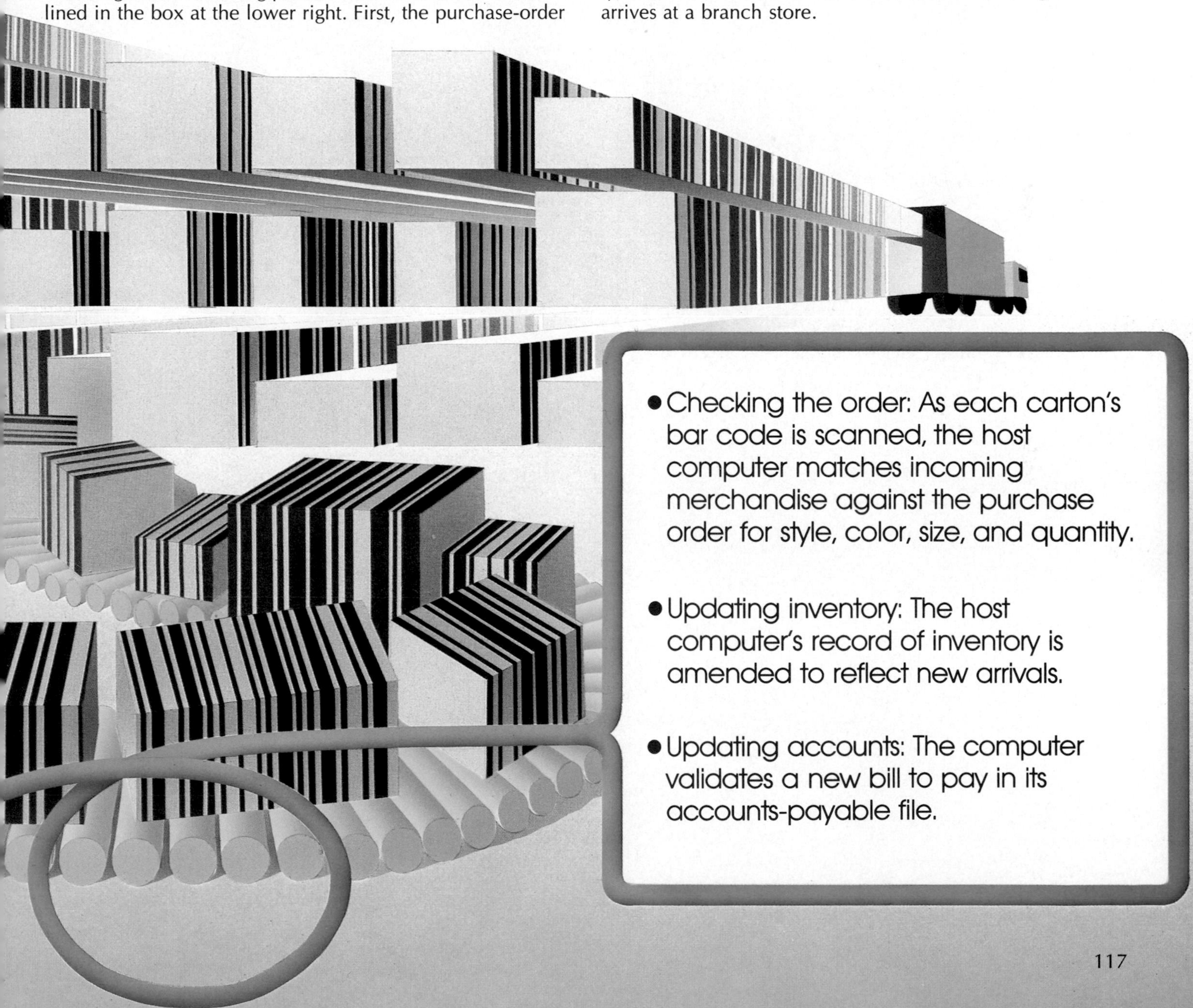

- Checking the order: As each carton's bar code is scanned, the host computer matches incoming merchandise against the purchase order for style, color, size, and quantity.

- Updating inventory: The host computer's record of inventory is amended to reflect new arrivals.

- Updating accounts: The computer validates a new bill to pay in its accounts-payable file.

A Revolution in Retailing

At the Terminal: Computerized Sales

To complete a sale in a fully automated department store, a clerk reads the bar code on the chosen item into the check-out terminal with a laser scanner similar to the one used on the receiving dock at headquarters. The bar-code data is relayed to the in-store processor, which looks up the product record for the item, sends its description and price back to the terminal, records details of the transaction, and notes the inventory change *(box, lower right).*

A terminal relieves the clerk of virtually all mental arithmetic. Tax is computed automatically, as are discounts, both sales and special ones such as those for senior citizens. When a customer buys one item from a prepackaged set, the terminal does the division. If cash is tendered, the terminal calculates the change. Other steps are also simplified. Authorization for credit comes automatically to the terminal from the in-store processor, which communicates with the headquarters' host computer for credit checks. And a special screen for the customer displays sales information; at some stores, the information also is announced in a synthesized voice. Completing a sale should take no more than a few seconds per item, speeding service to the customer while avoiding human error.

Because terminals are part of a larger network, they can be used for both intra- and interstore communications. A manager can help train new clerks by monitoring the operation of their terminals from another terminal in a separate office. And if a branch runs out of an item, a supervisor can locate stock either at another store or at the warehouse via the point-of-sale terminal that checks with the host computer at headquarters.

- Calculating the bill: The point-of-sale terminal adds the items purchased, displays the cost on the terminal screen, and, for cash or check sales, figures change.
- Updating accounts: If an article is charged, the customer's store credit account at headquarters is updated; if the sale is cash, the amount is noted as cash received. All sales are added to the accounts receivable records.
- Updating sales records: Information from each sale, such as time of day and type of payment, is filed.

At Day's End, a Complete Accounting

At the close of the business day, each branch store balances the registers. Cash, checks, and credit slips in the drawer at the terminals are added up and compared with their transaction records. Although the contents of drawers still must be counted manually, the in-store processor helps the clerks balance their accounts by providing subtotals for each terminal and each clerk by payment type.

The transfer of sales information from the branches to headquarters also usually takes place after business hours, though in some systems information is relayed periodically throughout the day. The host computer initiates and conducts this transfer, reading out of each in-store processor the data it has accumulated from the store's terminals (below). Once this information has been collected, the host computer gets to work, adjusting records and updating accounts for payroll and various types of sales.

In addition to these housekeeping chores, the central computer compiles numerous reports, many of which are sent

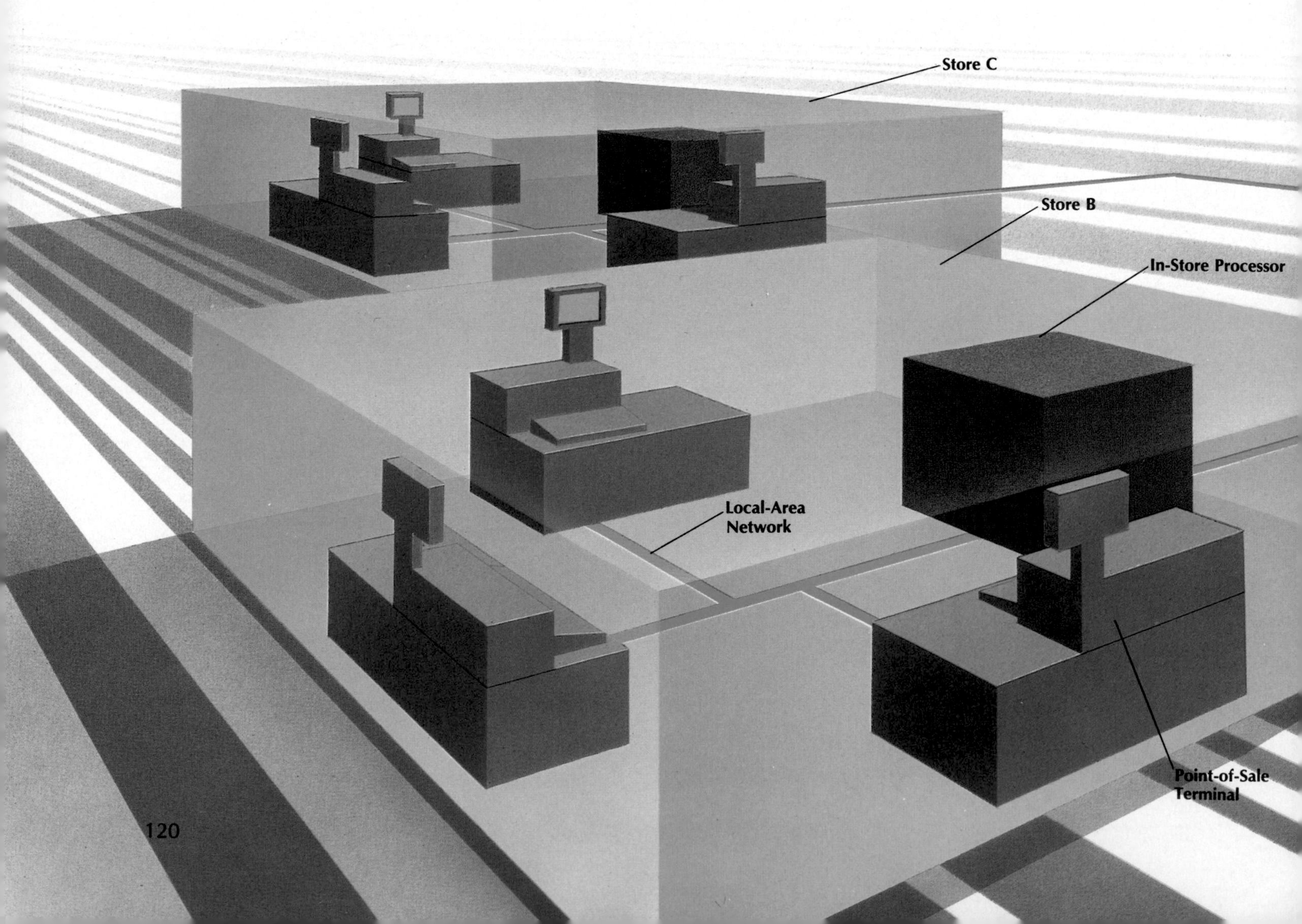

back to the branch stores. One type of report spotlights fast-selling items. Local managers consult it when allocating shelf space, and the chain's merchandise buyers rely on it to stay abreast of demand. A second sort of report breaks down sales activities by employee and time of day, allowing managers to evaluate the performance of individual clerks as well as to isolate peak hours when additional staff may be needed.

Other reports supplied by the host computer provide a wider view of operations and assist top managers. For example, one report may help assess the chain's credit policies by compiling the percentage of accounts that are paid up; if many of them are delinquent, management may tighten restrictions when evaluating applicants. Another report might pinpoint unusual events at a branch store, such as an inordinate number of transactions voided or a sudden surge in sales. Headquarters often compares the exception reports of the most and least successful stores to develop strategies for increasing profit.

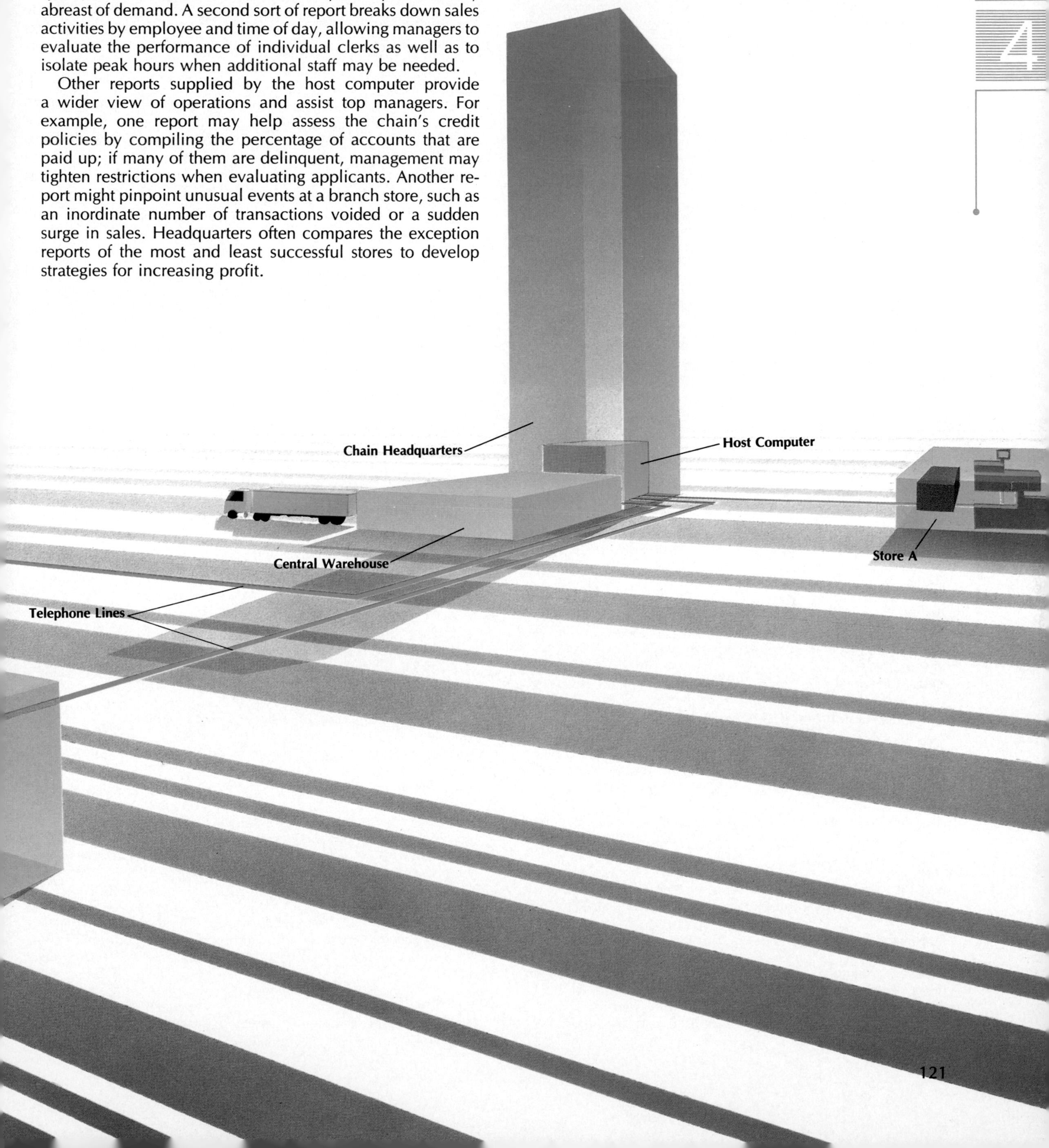

Chain Headquarters
Host Computer
Central Warehouse
Store A
Telephone Lines

Glossary

Algorithm: a step-by-step procedure for solving a problem.
Analog: the representation of a continuously changing physical variable (sound, for example) by another physical variable (such as electrical current).
Assembly language: a form of notation, specific to a given computer, in which a short mnemonic directly represents a specific instruction to the machine.
Attribute: a characteristic that describes an object in a relational data base. For instance, a collection of data about employees might contain an attribute column for employee identification number.
Audio response unit: a device that stores human speech fragments in digital form and then mixes and converts them into audible responses appropriate to commands received from another computer. Such audio devices work in conjunction with a host computer to provide, for example, banking services to customers over the telephone.
Automated clearinghouse (ACH): a computerized facility that sorts electronic payment transactions originating at many different banks into groups of payments, each of which is routed to a single bank.
Automated teller machine (ATM): a computer terminal used by bank customers for conducting routine transactions, such as deposits, withdrawals, or transfers of funds from one account to another.
Bar code: a series of dark bars and light spaces used to represent a number keyed to a computer file containing information, usually about an item of inventory.
Batch processing: a method of executing programs on a computer in which instructions and data are submitted to the computer at one time and the results are released when the entire job is complete.
Binary: having two components or possible states.
Binary code: a system for representing things by combinations of two symbols, such as one and zero, true and false, or the presence or absence of voltage.
Binary search: a technique for rapidly isolating the object of a search through a sequentially arranged data base by dividing it into successively smaller halves.
Bit: the smallest unit of information in a computer, represented by a single zero or one. The word "bit" is a contraction of "binary digit."
Buffer: a space reserved in a computer's memory for temporarily storing data, often en route to a peripheral device such as a printer or a monitor.
Byte: a sequence of eight bits treated as a unit for computation or storage.
Central processing unit (CPU): the part of a computer that executes instructions.
Channels: small, special-purpose processors programmed with instructions that allow them to store and retrieve data in a computer's memory independently of the central processing unit.
Chip: *See* Integrated circuit.
Data base: a collection of facts about a particular subject or related subjects, divided into individual files and records that are organized for easy access.
Data-base administrator: an individual who works with an organization to tailor a data base to its needs, then controls the operation, maintenance, and protection of the data and data-base utility programs.
Data-base management system (DBMS): software that organizes and provides ready access to the information in a data base.
Data-base model: the structure by which a data-base management system establishes the relationships between data and presents this organization to the user. *See also* Data base; Relational data base.
Data bus: the wires in a computer that carry data to and from memory.
Data definition: the process of declaring data characteristics and relationships for a data base.
Data dictionary: reference information, usually stored in the data base, that lists and describes all of the categories within a data base.
Digital computer: a machine that operates on data expressed in discrete, or on-off, form rather than the continuous representation used in an analog computer.
Digitize: to represent data in digital, or discrete, form, or to convert an analog, or continuous, signal to such a form.
Disk: a round plate made of plastic, metal, or glass, and used for storing data either magnetically or optically.
Encryption: scrambling data or messages with a cipher or code so that they are unreadable without a secret key.
Fault-tolerance: the ability of a computer to continue processing despite the failure of any single hardware or software component.
Hierarchical data base: an organizational system resembling an inverted tree, with individual data-base records arranged into groups and subgroups.
Input: information fed into a computer.
Integrated circuit (IC): an electronic circuit whose components are formed on a single piece of semiconductor material, usually silicon; sometimes called a chip.
Interrupt: a temporary halt in executing a program, or the signal that causes the pause.
Job: the unit in which a user submits work to the computer system.
Local area network (LAN): a system of computer hardware and software that links computers, printers, and other peripherals into a network suitable for transmission of data between offices in a building, for example, or between buildings situated near one another.
Machine code: a set of binary digits that can be directly understood by the computer without translation.
Magnetic tape: plastic tape coated on one side with a magnetic material that stores information as varying patterns of magnetization.
Mainframe computer: the largest type of computer, usually capable of serving many users simultaneously.
Memory: the principal area within a computer for storing instructions and data, typically composed of integrated circuits capable of holding thousands or millions of bits apiece.
Memory chip: a chip whose components form thousands of cells, each holding a single bit of information.
Microcomputer: a desktop or portable computer, based on a microprocessor and meant for a single user; often called a home or personal computer.
Microprocessor: a single chip containing all the elements of a computer's central processing unit.
Minicomputer: a midsized computer smaller than a mainframe and usually with more memory than a microcomputer.
Mnemonic: a short but memorable designation for a computer instruction or operation, such as "pr" for "print."
Modem: the abbreviation for modulator/demodulator, a device that enables data to be transmitted between computers, generally over telephone lines.
Multiprogramming: the apparently simultaneous operation of several programs that are loaded together into a computer's memory.
Multitasking: the ability of an operating system to perform several functions in such quick succession that they seem to occur at the same time.
Occurrence: a single instance of information about an object in a data base.
On-line: any type of computer use in which a person has immediate,

continuous access to the machine's central processing unit and its main memory throughout a computing job. Generally refers to the technique of entering data and instruction directly into a computer.
On-line transaction processing (OLTP): the term commonly used to describe a technique in which a common data base is available to multiple users for retrieval and updates.
Operating system: a complex set of programs that controls, assists, and supervises the allocation of all computing resources—memory, CPU, and peripherals—as programs are run in a computer.
Output: the data presented by a computer either directly to the user, to another computer, or to some form of storage.
Page: the result of dividing a program or data into portions of equal size, each stored as a unit in memory, or on disk or tape.
Personal identification number (PIN): a unique number or code that a customer enters into an automated teller machine, for instance, to prove ownership of an account.
Photodetector: a device that senses light and converts it into an electrical signal.
Program: a sequence of detailed instructions for performing some operation or solving some problem by computer.
Programming language: a set of words, letters, numerals, and abbreviated mnemonics, regulated by a rigid syntax, used to describe a program to a computer.
Random-access memory (RAM): a form of temporary memory whose contents can be altered by the user and that provides direct, rather than serial, access to stored information.
Read-only memory (ROM): permanent internal memory containing data or operation instructions that cannot be altered.
Record: the basic organizational unit of a data base, consisting of a group of facts about an object.
Relation: the mathematical name given to the arrangement of data into tables in a relational data base.
Relational data base: a data base that does not require predetermined relationships among individual records but can reveal unanticipated connections or establish new ones at any time.
Scanner: a device that senses the patterns of a code symbol and converts it to an electrical signal for digital processing.
Software: instructions, or programs, designed to be carried out by a computer.
Storage: devices such as disks and tapes that store data either magnetically or optically; though slower-working than a computer's internal electronic memory, storage devices provide virtually unlimited capacity and preserve data indefinitely.
Structured query language (SQL): an example of a computer language that is used to compose instructions for manipulating or locating information within a data base.
Subroutine: a self-contained section of a computer program that can be separately prepared, or prewritten program instructions for commonly used command sequences.
Table: *See* Relation.
Task: a single step of an operating-system job.
Time-sharing: the concurrent use of a computer by more than one person.
Transaction: the exchange of a piece of information between a computer and a human user.
Transistor: an electronic semiconductor device used as a switch or an amplifier.
Universal product code (UPC): a twelve-digit bar code used by grocery stores and other retailers. *See also* Bar code.
Vacuum tube: the earliest form of electronic switch, eventually replaced by transistors.
Virtual memory: a technique for handling programs too large to fit all at once into a computer's memory: programs and data are divided into pages or segments that are sorted on disk or tape and loaded into memory only as needed for the program's execution.
Word: a group of bits, ranging from four to sixty-four, treated as a unit by a computer and capable of being stored at a single memory address. *See also* Byte.

Bibliography

Books

Augarten, Stan, *Bit by Bit*. New York: Ticknor & Fields, 1984.
Bashe, C. J., et al., *IBM's Early Computers*. Cambridge: The MIT Press, 1986.
Belzer, J., A. G. Holzman, and A. Kent, *Encyclopedia of Computer Science and Technology*. New York: Marcel Dekker, 1975.
Calingaert, Peter, *Operating System Elements*. Englewood Cliffs, N. J.: Prentice-Hall, 1982.
Cannon, Don L., and Gerald Luecke, *Understanding Microprocessors*. Dallas, Tex.: Texas Instruments, 1984.
Date, C. J., *An Introduction to Database Systems*. Vol. 1. Reading, Mass.: Addison-Wesley, 1986.
Davies, Helen, and Mike Wharton, *Inside The Chip*. London: Usborne Publishing, 1983.
Fife, Dennis W., W. Terry Hardgrave, and Donald R. Deutsch, *Database Concepts*. Cincinnati: South-Western Publishing Company, 1986.
Fisher, Franklin M., James W. McKie, and Richard B. Mancke, *IBM and the U.S. Data Processing Industry*. New York: Praeger, 1983.
Fishman, Katharine Davis, *The Computer Establishment*. New York: Harper & Row, 1981.
Freiberger, Paul, and Michael Swaine, *Fire in the Valley*. Berkeley, Calif.: Osborne/McGraw-Hill, 1984.
Greenberger, Martin, ed., *Computers and the World of the Future*. Cambridge: The M.I.T. Press, 1962.
Harmon, C. K., and R. Adams, *Reading Between the Lines*. Peterborough, N. H.: North American Technology, 1984.
Janson, Philippe A., *Operating Systems Structures and Mechanisms*. London: Academic Press, 1985.
Kurzban, Stanley A., Thomas S. Heines, and Anthony P. Sayers, *Operating Systems Principles*. New York: Van Nostrand Reinhold, 1984.
Lipis, Allen H., Thomas R. Marschall, and Jan H. Linker, *Electronic Banking*. New York: Wiley, 1985.
Lister, A. M., *Fundamentals of Operating Systems*. New York: Springer-Verlag New York, 1984.
McClellan, Stephen T., *The Coming Computer Industry Shakeout*. New York: Wiley, 1984.
Mayall, W. H., *The Challenge of the Chip*. London: Her Majesty's Stationery Office, 1980.
Moreau, R., *The Computer Comes of Age*. Cambridge: The MIT Press, 1984.
Murtha, Stephen M., and Mitchell Waite, *CP/M Primer*. Indianapolis: Howard W. Sams, 1980.

Nikolaieff, George A., ed., *Computers and Society*. New York: H. W. Wilson, 1970.
Osborne, Adam, and David Bunnell, *An Introduction to Microcomputers: Volume 0, The Beginner's Book*. Berkeley, Calif.: Osborne/McGraw-Hill, 1982.
Peterson, James L., and Abraham Silberschatz, *Operating System Concepts*. Reading, Mass.: Addison-Wesley, 1983.
Ralston, Anthony, and Edwin D. Reilly, Jr., *Encyclopedia of Computer Science and Engineering*. New York: Van Nostrand Reinhold, 1983.
Rogers, Everett M., and Judith K. Larsen, *Silicon Valley Fever*. New York: Basic Books, 1984.
Sanders, Donald H., *Computers Today*. New York: McGraw-Hill, 1983.
Simon, John J., Jr., ed., *From Sand to Circuits and Other Inquiries*. Cambridge: Harvard University Office for Information Technology, 1986.
Tanenbaum, Andrew S., *Operating Systems*. Englewood Cliffs, N. J.: Prentice-Hall, 1987.
Turner, Raymond W., *Operating Systems*. New York: Macmillan, 1986.
Walker, Roger S., *Understanding Computer Science*. Fort Worth, Tex.: Radio Shack, 1981.
Williams, Michael R., *A History of Computing Technology*. Englewood Cliffs, N.J.: Prentice-Hall, 1985.
Williams, Trevor I., ed., *A History of Technology*, Vol. 7. Oxford, England: Clarendon Press, 1978.

Periodicals

Balderston, F. E., James M. Carman, and Austin C. Hoggatt, "Computers in Banking and Marketing." *Science*, Mar. 18, 1977.
Bashe, C. J., et al., "The Architecture of IBM's Early Computers." *IBM Journal of Research and Development*, Sept. 1981.
"The Breakdown of America's 'Tax Factories'." *The Washington Post*, Oct. 22, 1985.
Brody, Herb, "Revolution in Toyland." *High Technology*, June 1987.
Brown, Kim, "Specialized Tools, Availability Spur Growth of OLTP." *Computerworld*, Sept. 29, 1986.
Burck, Gilbert, "'On Line' in 'Real Time'." *Fortune*, April 1964.
Cane, Alan, "Doubts Have Evaporated." *Financial Times*, Sept. 29, 1986.
"Cautious Confidence at I.R.S." *The New York Times*, Feb. 20, 1986.
"A Computer That Won't Shut Down." *Business Week*, Dec. 8, 1975.
Connell, Charles, "Computers That Just Won't Quit." *High Technology*, Dec. 1986.
Creer, Richard, "TP Evolution: How Customer Information Control System Splashed out of the Swamp." *The IBM USER*, March 1982.
Cronin, Michael A., "Fifty Years of Operations in the Social Security Administration." *Social Security Bulletin*, June 1985.
Dataquest, Inc., "On-Line Transaction Processing, Why is This Market Growing?" *Research Newsletter*, 1986-33, San Jose, Calif., Dataquest, Inc. 1986.
Davis, Dwight B., "Artificial Intelligence Goes to Work." *High Technology*, April 1987.
Denning, Peter J., and Robert L. Brown, "Operating Systems." *Scientific American*, Sept. 1984.
Dickinson, John, "Fault Tolerance Goes Mainframe." *Computers in Banking*, Sept. 1986.
Dunn, Si, "Super SABRE." *American Way*, Sept. 1984.
Dworetzky, Tom, "Taxing Times for the I.R.S." *Discover*, May 1986.
Economic Review, "Federal Reserve Bank of Atlanta." April 1986.
"Electronic Banking." *Business Week*, Jan. 18, 1982.
Evans, B. O., "System/360: A Retrospective View." *Annals of the History of Computing*, April 1986.
Evans, George J., Jr., "Experience Gained from the American Airlines SABRE System Control Program." *Proceedings A.C.M. National Meeting*, 1967.
"Excellence in Management Awards." *Industry Week*, Oct. 15, 1984.
Gannon, Robert, "Big-Brother 7074 is Watching You." *Popular Science* , March 1963.
Garetz, Mark, "Evolution of the Microprocessor." *BYTE*, Sept. 1985.
Gill, Philip J., "On-line Transaction Processing." *Computerworld*, Sept. 29, 1986.
Glaser, E. L., and F. J. Corbato, "Introduction to Time-Sharing." *Datamation*, Nov. 1964.
Godwin, Jim, "A Simple, Low-Cost Scanner." *Laser Focus Magazine*, Oct. 1981.
Grafton, William P., "IMS: Past, Present, Future." *Datamation*, Sept. 1983.
Hamilton F. E., and E. C. Kubie, "The IBM Magnetic Drum Calculator Type 650." *Annals of the History of Computing*, Jan. 1986.
Howe, Charles, "The FT Crowd." *Datamation*, May 15, 1985.
Hurd, Cuthbert C., ed., "Special Issue: IBM 701 Thirtieth Anniversary." *Annals of the History of Computing*, April 1983.
IBM Systems Journal. Vol. 16, No. 2. International Business Machines Corporation, 1977.
"Information Power." *Business Week*, Oct. 14, 1985.
Kador, John, "What's Ahead for CICS." *Datamation*, Sept. 1, 1986.
Knight, John R., "A Case Study: Airlines Reservations Systems." *Proceedings of the IEEE*, Vol. 60, Nov. 1972.
Korzeniowski, Paul, "Tandem Beats Up On Big Blue." *Network World*, Sept. 22, 1986.
Levine, Jonathan B., "How Jim Treybig Whipped Tandem Back into Shape." *Business Week*, Feb. 23, 1987.
McCarthy, John, "Information." *Scientific American*, Sept. 1966.
Main, Jeremy, "Computer Time-Sharing—Everyman at the Console." *Fortune*, August 1967.
Murphy, Jamie, "Glitches and Crashes at the IRS." *Time*, April 29, 1985.
"The New Computerized Age." *Saturday Review*, July 23, 1966.
"New Strength for EDP." *Oasis*, Nov. 1961.
"New Tax Detective: A Gimlet-eyed Machine." *Business Week*, Feb. 8, 1964.
"'On-Line' Systems Sweep the Computer World." *Business Week*, July 14, 1986.
O'Reilly, Brian, "How Jimmy Treybig Turned Tough." *Fortune*, May 25, 1987.
Rosin, Robert F., "Supervisory and Monitor Systems." *Computing Surveys*, March 1969.
Rosin, Robert F., ed., "Prologue: The Burroughs B 5000." *Annals of the History of Computing*. 1987.
"SABRE, a $30-Million Application." *Fortune*, April 1964.
"SABRE—Realtime Benchmark Has the Winning Ticket." *Data*

Management, Sept. 1981.
Serlin, Omri, "Fault Tolerant Blues." *Datamation,* Mar. 15, 1985.
Sheehan, Michael, "Paint by Computers." *Network World,* May 19, 1986.
Taylor, A., "Testing Time for the Tax Collectors." *Fortune,* April 14, 1986.
Trimble, George R., "The IBM 650 Magnetic Drum Calculator." *Annals of the History of Computing,* Jan. 1986.
Yelavich, B. M., "Customer Information Control System—An Evolving System Facility." *IBM Systems Journal.* 1985.
Zani, Ralph L., and William M. Zani, "Towards the Computer Utility: Evolution or Revolution." *Datamation,* October 1969.

Other Sources

About the Universal Product Code. Dayton: Uniform Code Council, 1986.
Annual Report 1986. New York: MasterCard International, Dec. 1986.
"Application Report: On-Line Transaction Processing Update." *InfoCorp,* Feb. 28, 1987.
Background Information: Tandem in Manufacturing. Cupertino, Calif.: Tandem Computers, Oct. 1986.
Background Information: Tandem in the Finance Industry, Cupertino, Calif.: Tandem Computers, Aug. 1986.
Bar Code. Cary, N.C.: DATALOGIC, no date.
Becker, Patricia A., "An Overview of Fault-Tolerant Systems." *Data Processing Management.* New York: Auerbach, 1986.
Braddock, Richard S., *New Era in Bank Marketing.* New York: Citicorp, Nov. 11, 1985.
Brown, R. R., and P. Nordyke, "ICS-An Information Control System." *North American Rockwell,* 1967.
Brown, R. H., *Office Automation Government.* New York: Automation Consultants. 1959.
Center: Commemorating Tandem's First Ten Years. Cupertino, Calif.: Tandem Computers, Winter 1986.
"Commonwealth Edison Company Customer Information System Using the IBM 2260 Display Station." *IBM Application Brief,* no date.
Communications Division. New York City Police Department Printing Section, no date.
"Computer Technology at IRS: Present and Planned." Washington, D.C.: U.S. General Accounting Office, Sept. 1983.
Datapro Reports on Banking Automation. Delran, N.J.: Datapro Research, 1987.
Datapro Reports on Retail Automation. Delran, N. J.: Datapro Research, 1987.
Fault Tolerant Processor Concepts and Operation. Delran, N.J.: Datapro Research, April 1985.
Introduction To Retailing: Self Instruction Course. Dayton: NCR Corporation, no date.
Introduction to Tandem Computer Systems. Cupertino, Calif.: Tandem Computers, Dec. 1983.
Mapstone, Robina, "Interview with Bob Patrick." Washington, D.C.: Smithsonian Computer History Project. Feb. 26, 1973.
"On-Line Transaction Processing: Why Is This Market Growing?" *Research Newsletter.* San Jose, Calif.: Dataquest, Sept. 1986.
Patrick, Robert L., "General Motors/North American Monitor for the IBM 704 Computer." Rand Corporation P-7316, Jan. 1987.
Plugge, W. R., and M. N. Perry, "American Airlines' 'SABRE' Electronic Reservations System." *Proceedings of the Western Joint Computer Conference,* Papers Presented at the Joint IRE-AIEE-ACM Computer Conference, Los Angeles, May 1961.
Scanning Products on the Move, Part III: Fixed Beam Scanners. Pittsburgh, Pa.: Automatic Identification Manufacturers, 1983.
Scanning Products on the Move Part I: Moving Beam Scanners. Pittsburgh: Automatic Identification Manufacturers, 1983.
7000 MMRS: An Executive Overview. Dayton: NCR Corporation, 1986.
Sumner, Bill:
"Bullock's UPC Success Story." Paper Presented at VICS Conference, Dallas, March 10, 1987.
"VICS Vendor Marking Subcommittee." Paper Presented at VICS Conference, Dallas, Tex., March 10, 1987.
"S.W.I.F.T. Profile." La Hulpe, Belgium: Society for WorldwideInterbank Financial Telecommunication, no date.
Tandem: Company Background Information. Cupertino, Calif.: Tandem Computers, Nov. 1986.
Telephone Electric Check System. Sunwest Federal Credit Union, Phoenix, no date.
UPC Code and Symbol Information Sheet. Dayton: Uniform Code Council, 1987.
UPC History Information Sheet. Dayton: Uniform Code Council, 1987.
UPC Symbol Scanning Information Sheet. Dayton: Uniform Code Council, 1987.
UPC Symbol Specification Manual. Dayton: Uniform Code Council, 1986.

Acknowledgments

The index for this book was prepared by Mel Ingber. The editors also wish to thank the following individuals and institutions: **In the United States:** California—Cupertino: Pat Becker and Joyce Strand, Tandem Computers Incorporated; Fullerton: Robert R. Brown; Los Altos Hills: Marcian "Ted" Hoff; Los Angeles: William Sumner, EDP Bullock's; Monterey: Gayle Steiner, Digital Research Inc.; San Francisco: Dennis Anglin and Dave Brancoli, VISA U.S.A.; San Jose: Kimball Brown, Dataquest; San Mateo: Daniel Brigham, VISA International; Santa Monica: Jack Campbell; Connecticut—Hartford: John S. Rydz, Emhart Corporation; District of Columbia: Electronic Funds Transfer Association; Eugene Snider, Federal Reserve Board of Governors; Larry Batdorf and Wilson Fadely, Internal Revenue Service; Illinois—Chicago: Todd Bolen, Commonwealth Edison; Maryland—Baltimore: Michael A. Cronin, James Dean, and Larry DeWitt, Social Security Administration; Chevy Chase: Robert Chartrand; Massachusetts—Cambridge: Fernando Corbato, Robert Fano, and Stuart Madnick, Massachusetts Institute of Technology; Canton: Alfred MacTavish and Pegi Wille, Computer Identics Corporation; Marlboro: Mike Grady, Stratus Computer, Inc.; Newton: Jonathan Titus, EDN; Missouri—St. Louis: Ronald W. Peterson, MasterCard International; New Jersey—Delran: Joseph Valente, Datapro Research Corporation; Fairfield: Jack Wurst, SSMC; New York—Armonk: Cal Braunstein, Malcolm Robinson, and Mark Root, IBM; Bohemia: Terry Meehan, Perifonics Corporation; New York: Deborah Hughes, MasterCard International; James S. Cannon, New York Police Department; Carl E. Brickman, Society for Worldwide

Interbank Financial Telecommunication (S.W.I.F.T.); Rye Brook: Tom Belz, IBM; Valhalla: Robert Polorak, IBM; Yorktown Heights: John H. Palmer, Thomas J. Watson Research Center; North Carolina—Cary: George Stevenson, DATALOGIC, Inc.; Charlotte: Michael Hoseman, Interstate Securities Corporation; Ohio—Dayton: Cynthia A. Bergevin and Robert Farkis, NCR Corporation; Sharon Focht, Uniform Code Council, Inc.; Oregon—Eugene: Brad Reddersen, Spectra-Physics Retail Systems; Tennessee—Memphis: Chris Demos, David C. Dietzel, and Armond Schneider, Federal Express Corporation; Moira Thornett, Holiday Corporation; Dewayne Bolton, M-Tech; Texas—Fort Worth: Max Hopper, John Hotard, and Joe Stroop, American Airlines; Virginia—McLean: John Stevenson, UNISYS Corporation; Richmond: Marian L. Swain, Federal Reserve Bank of Richmond, Virginia.

Picture Credits

The sources for the illustrations that appear in this book are listed below. Credits from left to right are separated by semicolons, from top to bottom by dashes.

Cover, 6: Art by Jeffrey Oh. 10, 11: Art by Alvin Pagan. 12-21: Art by Jeffrey Oh. 25-37: Art by Stephen Wagner. 38: Art by Jeffrey Oh. 42, 43: Art by Sharon Cohen. 46-51: Art by Jeffrey Oh. 53-63: Art by Al Kettler. 64: Art by Jeffrey Oh. 68, 69: Art by Lili Robins. 72, 77: Art by Jeffrey Oh. 79-87: Art by Peter Sawyer of Design Innovations. 88: Art by Jeffrey Oh. 92-97: Art by Mark Robinson. 100: Art by Jeffrey Oh. 104-107: Art by Mark Robinson. 111: Art by Jeffrey Oh. 113-121: Art by Steve Bauer/Bill Burrows & Associates.

Index

Numerals in italics indicate an illustration of the subject mentioned.

UNDERSTANDING COMPUTERS

SERIES DIRECTOR: Lee Hassig
Series Administrator: Loretta Britten

Editorial Staff for *The Computerized Society*
Designer: Christopher M. Register
Associate Editors: Susan V. Kelly (pictures), Lydia Preston, principal, Thomas H. Flaherty (text)
Researchers: Roxie France-Nuriddin, Tina S. McDowell, Pamela L. Whitney
Writer: Robert M. S. Somerville
Assistant Designers: Paul M. Graboff, Sue Deal-Daniels
Editorial Assistant: Miriam P. Newton
Copy Coordinator: Elizabeth Graham
Picture Coordinator: Renée DeSandies

Special Contributors: Mark A. Bello, Elisabeth Carpenter, David Darling, Martin Mann, John I. Merritt, Ken Sheldon, Don Sider, Charles C. Smith (text), Susan Calhoun, Ann Dusel Corson (research)

CONSULTANTS

STUART R. BLOOM has more than fourteen years' experience as a computer consultant. Presently, he is employed by Carmody & Company, Inc., a management consulting firm to the financial services industry.

LIAM CARMODY is a senior partner of Carmody & Company. With nearly two decades' experience in the financial service industry, Mr. Carmody is known nationally as a pioneer in the field of electronic banking.

DENNIS W. FIFE, an adjunct faculty member at George Washington University, has a Ph.D in electrical engineering. His professional experiences have focused on data-base design and testing for commercial and defense applications.

RUSSEL HOYLE is head of Product Management for NCR Corporation. He has extensive experience with information- and transaction-processing computer systems serving the needs of financial and retail markets worldwide.

DONALD G. LONG, a director of the Electronic Funds Transfer Association, is a finance industry consultant with IBM. His banking-related positions at IBM have included sales of mainframe computers to major New York banks, and product management of automated teller machines and financial services terminals.

FREDERICK B. MAXWELL, a microcomputer specialist, is currently working at ADEC, Inc., an energy management and conservation company.

BERT MOORE is manager for Technical Communications with Automatic Identification Manufacturers, Inc. (AIM), the trade association of organizations that manufacture automatic identification equipment such as bar-code scanners.

ISABEL LIDA NIRENBERG has dealt with a wide range of computer applications, from the analysis of data collected by the Pioneer space probes to the matching of children and families for adoption agencies. She works in the Computer Center of the State University of New York at Albany.

ROBERT L. PATRICK has been an independent computer specialist since 1959 in the fields of systems analysis and design for business, industry, and government.

BOB UNANSKI joined Tandem Computers, Inc., in November of 1975 as manager of Software Education. He is presently Program Manager for Telemarketing at Tandem.

MARK WEISER is an associate professor in the Computer Science Department at the University of Maryland, where he also serves as Associate Chairman for Facilities. Noted for his design of software windows, he is interested in environments for heterogeneous systems.

Library of Congress Cataloging in Publication Data

The Computerized society / by the editors of Time-Life Books.
p. cm.--(Understanding computers)
Bibliography: p.
Includes index.
ISBN 0-8094-5720-2.
1. Computers and civilization. 2. Electronic digital computers.
I. Time-Life Books. II. Series.
QA76.9.C66C638 1987 303.4'834—dc19 87-18169
CIP

ISBN 0-8094-5721-0 (lib. bdg.)

For information on and a full description of any of the Time-Life Books series listed, please write:
Reader Information
Time-Life Customer Service
P.O. Box C-32068
Richmond, Virginia 23261-2068

First printing. Printed in U.S.A.
Published simultaneously in Canada.
School and library distribution by Silver Burdett Company, Morristown, New Jersey.